# *the after-work*
# THAI
# COOKBOOK

# the after-work
# THAI
## COOKBOOK

how to rustle up an exotic supper in an instant,
with over 65 fast, simple and delicious recipes

BECKY JOHNSON

southwater

This edition is published by Southwater

Southwater is an imprint of Anness Publishing Ltd
Hermes House, 88–89 Blackfriars Road, London SE1 8HA
tel. 020 7401 2077; fax 020 7633 9499
www.southwaterbooks.com; www.annesspublishing.com

If you like the images in this book and would like to investigate using them for
publishing, promotions or advertising, please visit our website www.practicalpictures.com
for more information.

© Anness Publishing Ltd 2005, 2006

UK agent: The Manning Partnership Ltd, 6 The Old Dairy, Melcombe Road, Bath BA2 3LR;
tel. 01225 478444; fax 01225 478440; sales@manning-partnership.co.uk

UK distributor: Grantham Book Services Ltd, Isaac Newton Way, Alma Park Industrial Estate,
Grantham, Lincs NG31 9SD; tel. 01476 541080; fax 01476 541061; orders@gbs.tbs-ltd.co.uk

North American agent/distributor: National Book Network, 4501 Forbes Boulevard, Suite 200,
Lanham, MD 20706; tel. 301 459 3366; fax 301 429 5746; www.nbnbooks.com

Australian agent/distributor: Pan Macmillan Australia, Level 18, St Martins Tower, 31 Market St,
Sydney, NSW 2000; tel. 1300 135 113; fax 1300 135 103; customer.service@macmillan.com.au

New Zealand agent/distributor: David Bateman Ltd, 30 Tarndale Grove, Off Bush Road, Albany,
Auckland; tel. (09) 415 7664; fax (09) 415 8892

Publisher: Joanna Lorenz
Managing Editor: Linda Fraser
Senior Editor: Susannah Blake
Photographer: Nicki Dowey
Food Stylist: Lucy McKelvie
Stylist: Helen Trent
Designer: Nigel Partridge
Jacket Designer: Balley Design Associates
Production Controller: Darren Price

Previously published as part of a larger volume, *Thai Food and Cooking*

10 9 8 7 6 5 4 3 2 1

**NOTES**
For all recipes, quantities are given in both metric and imperial measures and, where appropriate,
measures are also given in standard cups and spoons. Follow one set, but not a mixture, because they
are not interchangeable.

Standard spoon and cup measures are level.
1 tsp = 5ml, 1 tbsp = 15ml, 1 cup = 250ml/8fl oz

Australian standard tablespoons are 20ml. Australian readers should use 3 tsp in place of 1 tbsp for
measuring small quantities of gelatine, cornflour, salt, etc.

Medium (US large) eggs are used unless otherwise stated.

Bracketed terms are intended for American readers.

# CONTENTS

# INTRODUCTION

The Thai cuisine is one of the jewels of the East, with its fiery flavours sitting in perfect harmony with subtle, fragrant aromas, sweet, creamy sauces and fresh, crunchy textures. Once tasted, all other cuisines seem to pale into insignificance.

In the last few years, the popularity of Thai food and cooking has grown enormously. With improved transport and lower air fares, more and more people are visiting Thailand and are able to experience the cuisine at first hand. Restaurants serving excellent, authentic Thai dishes have become commonplace. Classic Thai ingredients such as lemon grass and kaffir lime leaves that were once hard to find and had to be sought out in specialist Asian stores are now available in most large supermarkets – opening up a wealth of possibilities to the home cook.

Another reason for Thai food's growing popularity is that it is perfectly suited to busy, modern lives. The majority of Thai dishes can be cooked quickly and use healthy cooking methods such as grilling (broiling), steaming, stir-frying and braising. Fresh vegetables, healthy fish and shellfish, tofu and low-fat cuts of meat and poultry are used in savoury dishes, and desserts are often fruit-based. Vegetables and fruit are usually raw or lightly cooked so they retain their taste, texture and valuable nutrients.

Not only are dishes quick and healthy, they can often be made using just one pan. The wok, which is the most useful vessel for Thai cooking, is so versatile that it can be used for frying, steaming and simmering. This means that you can use the wok to cook whole dishes, which will save time on washing up after dinner.

## THE SECRET OF THE THAI CUISINE

Thai cooking relies on the use of the "five flavours": salty, sweet, sour, bitter and hot. Salty flavourings such as soy sauce, Thai fish sauce, shrimp paste and oyster sauce help to bring out the flavours of the other ingredients. Sweet ingredients such as palm sugar and coconut milk help to enhance the flavour of herbs and spices in savoury dishes. Sour flavourings such as lime juice, tamarind and rice vinegar help to accentuate other flavours. The bitter taste, which is introduced through the addition of herbs and green vegetables, is balanced against the other four flavours. The main source of heat is chilli – either fresh, dried, in pastes or in sauces – but heat is also introduced through ginger, onions and garlic.

It is the perfect balance of these five elements that gives Thai food its distinctive character. Each recipe in this book utilizes the basic principle of the five flavours to create fabulous, authentic dishes that will transport you to another world.

### EATING THAI-STYLE

In Thailand, meals are a time for family and friends to gather together, share food and enjoy. Foods can be separated into savoury and sweet, but within this distinction dishes are usually served together rather than as several separate courses. A traditional Thai meal will usually consist of clear soup served with steamed rice, a steamed or braised dish, a fried dish, a salad and a spicy sauce. The dishes should offer a range of different tastes and textures, creating a perfect harmony of flavours. Fresh fruit is typically served after the meal, but there are also more elaborate sweet dishes based on fruit and coconut that are utterly delicious.

### STRESS-FREE SHORTCUTS

If you're in a real hurry, there are plenty of shortcuts for many of the recipes in this book. Spice pastes are traditionally pounded by hand in a mortar but you can cut many minutes of preparation time by whizzing the ingredients

*Left: You can serve fragrant chicken curry with plain boiled rice for a simple meal, or as part of a selection of dishes for a more traditional Thai feast.*

*Above: These egg rolls with herbs and chilli look very pretty and are surprisingly easy to make.*

together in a food processor. Curry pastes can also be made in advance and stored in an airtight container in the refrigerator until ready to use. (If even this seems like too much effort, you can buy excellent ready-made Thai pastes in most large supermarkets – so add some jars to the store cupboard.)

When you buy fish or shellfish, ask the fishmonger to clean and prepare it for you so you can just take it home and cook it. After all, no one should have to prepare squid, or fillet a fish, after a long, hard day at work. The same is true when buying meat and poultry. Ask the butcher to prepare cuts of meat to save you time once you get home.

Think about the whole meal before you start preparing ingredients. Decide what you want to eat, then look at the recipes and see how long each one is going to take. If something needs to stand for 10 or 20 minutes – work this into your preparation time. If you're missing a key ingredient, choose a different recipe. If a dessert needs to be chilled for an hour or two, make this first then put it in the refrigerator while you make the rest of the meal. Planning and forethought are the simplest ways to guarantee stress-free, perfect results and a relaxing few hours when you get home from work.

## ABOUT THIS BOOK

This book is devoted to helping you enjoy the taste of authentic Thai cooking, even when time is short. Each recipe should take less than 30 minutes to prepare, and they have been grouped into six easy-to-use chapters so that you can pick the right dish in an instant. You can choose a selection of dishes to create a more traditional-style Thai meal – or a single main dish served with simple boiled rice or noodles.

If you have a little more time on your hands, there is a fabulous selection of appetizers to munch on. Some, such as crispy rice cakes and roasted coconut cashew nuts, can be prepared in advance so you can save time by making them the night before. However, even the more complex snacks, such as corn fritters, aubergine (eggplant) and pepper tempura, and pretty egg rolls, are still quick and simple to make.

The desserts are quick and easy to prepare, too. Cold desserts can be made before the main course and then chilled until ready to serve, while the hot desserts take very little time to make. The batter for coconut pancakes can be whisked together in no time at all and takes only minutes to cook, while the custard for filling nectarines can be prepared before the meal and steamed at the last minute.

*Below: Traditional Thai desserts are often based on fruit and make a refreshing finish to a meal.*

# THE MAIN INGREDIENTS

Thai cuisine is based on simple, fresh ingredients. Many, such as fresh root ginger, garlic and soy sauce, will be familiar to most Western cooks, but there are other ingredients that may be less well-known. This section looks at all the classic ingredients needed to create authentic Thai food, with tips on buying, preparing and cooking.

## ESSENTIAL FLAVOURINGS

The secret of Thai cooking is the judicious use of flavourings – from fresh herbs, spices and aromatics to sour lime juice, sweet palm sugar and fragrant jasmine flowers.

### Basil

Three different types of basil are used in Thai cooking: Thai, holy and lemon. Thai basil has a sweet, aniseed flavour and is used in red curries. It is similar in appearance to Western sweet basil, which can be used as a substitute. Holy, or hot, basil has a pungent flavour and is used with fish, poultry and beef. Lemon basil is a small, delicate variety that is rarely found outside Asia. In Thailand, it is used in soups and sprinkled over salads.

### Mint

Fresh mint is a popular flavouring in Thai cooking, particularly in salads.

*Below: Fresh root ginger is an essential ingredient in Thai cooking, adding a fresh, peppery flavour to many dishes.*

*Above: Holy basil has dull green leaves and a much stronger flavour than Western sweet basil.*

### Chives

Long, thin chives have a delicate onion flavour and are often used as a garnish. Chinese, or garlic, chives are bigger than the Western variety and have a much stronger, more garlicky flavour.

### Coriander/Cilantro

The whole coriander plant – leaves, roots and seeds – is used in Thai cooking. The fragrant leaves are used in soups, sauces and curries and as a garnish. The fresh herb is very delicate so should be used as soon as possible after purchase. The roots are crushed and used for marinades; they will keep for several days in the refrigerator. The round brown seeds have a warm, aromatic flavour and are used in curry pastes. They can be stored in an airtight container for many months. The ground spice loses its flavour quickly so it is better to buy whole seeds and grind them as and when required.

### Ginger

This knobbly root has a papery, brown skin covering the firm, fresh, zesty, peppery flesh. The skin is removed, then the flesh is sliced, chopped or pounded to a paste and used in curries, stir-fries, soups, salads and marinades. It can be stored, wrapped, in the refrigerator for up to 2 weeks.

### Galangal

This knobbly rhizome is a member of the ginger family and has a similar appearance. There are two varieties: greater and lesser galangal. The latter is favoured in Thai cooking. Its flavour is a cross between fresh root ginger and black pepper and it is often used in jungle curries and with fish. It is prepared and used in much the same way as fresh root ginger. Fresh galangal is available in Asian stores and can be stored, wrapped, in the refrigerator for up to 2 weeks.

### Lemon grass

This slightly woody, pale green stem is an essential Thai flavouring. It is used in savoury dishes and desserts to impart a delicate citrus flavour. The fibrous layers surrounding the stalk are generally removed, then the fleshy bulbous end of the stalk shredded or pounded to a paste. The whole stalk, or just the upper portion, may be lightly bruised with a pestle and used to flavour stocks. Fresh lemon grass stalks are sold in bunches in supermarkets and Asian stores. Dried and bottled chopped lemon grass are a poor substitute for the fresh herb.

### Coconut

This large, brown, hairy nut is an essential ingredient in Thai cooking – used both for its flavour and its rich creamy consistency. Coconut milk, cream, shredded fresh coconut and desiccated (dry unsweetened) coconut are widely used in both sweet and savoury dishes. When choosing fresh coconuts, select nuts that feel heavy; when you shake them you should be able to hear liquid sloshing about inside. Coconut milk and cream are available in cans and cartons; desiccated coconut is available in packets. Blocks of creamed coconut are also sometimes available, and can be grated and reconstituted using a little boiling water.

*Above: Fragrant, zesty lemon grass is one of the essential flavours used in both sweet and savoury Thai dishes.*

## Garlic

This pungent member of the onion family is used extensively in Thai cooking. Thai garlic has a pinkish skin and tends to be more potent than Western varieties. Small bulbs of garlic preserved in sweet and sour brine are also a popular flavouring and condiment and are available from Asian stores. Garlic oil has a pleasant aroma of garlic and is used to impart a delicate flavour to dishes; it is available from Asian stores and supermarkets.

## Kaffir lime leaves

These dark green, shiny leaves are an essential flavouring in many Thai dishes. The leaves are usually torn or shredded before adding to a dish to release their distinctive citrus flavour. To shred leaves, cut out the tough stem, then roll the leaf into a tight scroll and slice. The leaves are available in most large supermarkets and Asian stores.

## Chillies

Fiery chillies are an essential part of most savoury Thai dishes. Fresh, dried or infused in oil, they are used to add heat and flavour to salads, soups, stir-fries, curries, pickles and sauces. Tiny red and green bird's eye chillies are extremely hot and much favoured in Thai cooking. Long, or cayenne, chillies

are milder than bird's eye ones. They are often used as a garnish, or dried and used in red curry paste. Dried chillies are also widely used – whole or crushed – and may be roasted to heighten their flavour before adding to dishes. Crushed dried chillies are offered as a condiment at the table and sprinkled over food to taste.

Much of the heat of chillies is contained in the seeds and white membranes surrounding the seeds so it is wise to remove these, unless you prefer your dishes fiery-hot. Chillies contain capsaicin, which can cause intense irritation to the skin and eyes, so always wash your hands with soap and water immediately after handling, or wear rubber (latex) gloves when preparing chillies.

## Peppercorns

Before chillies were introduced to Thailand in the 16th century, pepper was used to add heat to dishes. Today, white peppercorns, which have a much milder flavour than black, are used for seasoning. Green peppercorns, which are the unripe berries, have a less complex flavour than white, and are used as a garnish for jungle curries and stir-fries. They are available fresh or bottled in brine: bottled ones should be drained and rinsed before use.

*Below: Blisteringly hot red and green bird's eye chillies are used to add heat and flavour to many Thai dishes.*

*Above: Turmeric is a glorious yellow-orange colour but the juice can stain, so handle it with care.*

## Turmeric

The fresh spice resembles fresh root ginger but has bright orange-yellow flesh. It has a peppery aroma and slightly musky flavour and is often used in curry pastes. The dried spice is the same bright yellow colour and is usually available ground. (The dried root is sometimes available, but it is very hard and difficult to grind.) Fresh turmeric is available from Asian stores and can be stored, wrapped, in the refrigerator for up to 2 weeks.

## Cumin

Ground cumin is often used in curry pastes. Once ground, the spice loses its aroma quickly, so it is best to buy whole seeds, then grind them in a mortar or spice grinder as you need them.

## Fennel

These small, brown, oval seeds have a slightly aniseedy flavour. They are often used ground in savoury dishes.

## Five-spice powder

This classic Chinese spice blend is a mixture of Sichuan peppercorns, cinnamon, cloves, fennel seeds and star anise and has a warm, fragrant aroma. It is very popular in Thailand and goes particularly well with duck, pork and beef.

### Tamarind

Commonly used as a souring agent to bring out and enhance the flavour of other ingredients, tamarind has a fruity, sharp taste, not unlike sour dates. Fresh tamarind pods are common in Asia, but you are more likely to find blocks of compressed tamarind or tubs of tamarind paste in the West. To use compressed tamarind, soak about 15ml/1 tbsp in 150ml/¼ pint/⅔ cup warm water for 10 minutes, then stir to release the pulp and strain the juice through a sieve. Discard the pulp remaining in the sieve and stir the juice into the dish. To use tamarind paste, simply mix with a little warm water, then add to the dish.

### Limes

Sharp, tangy limes are widely used in Thai dishes and add the essential sour flavour to sweet and savoury dishes. The sourness of the juice brings out the flavours of other ingredients and is used to balance the intense sweetness of many fruits and desserts.

### Rice vinegar

Made from fermented rice, this vinegar has a sharp, tangy flavour and is used to add a sour element to many Thai dishes. It is available from Asian stores and large supermarkets.

*Below: Palm sugar is usually available in blocks and can vary in colour from pale gold to light brown.*

*Above: The tart, fruity pulp found inside tamarind pods is used as a souring agent in many Thai dishes.*

### Sesame oil

This strongly flavoured, nutty, brown oil is used for flavouring rather than cooking. It is generally sprinkled over food just before serving. It is available from supermarkets and Asian stores.

### Mekhong whisky

This potent rice whisky is similar to bourbon in flavour. It may be enjoyed as a drink, but is also used as a flavouring in dishes such as jungle curry.

### Palm sugar

Also known as jaggery, palm sugar is made from the sap of various palms. It varies from light to deep golden brown, has a crumbly texture and is usually available in blocks. It has a distinctive flavour and is slightly less sweet than cane sugar. To use, grate off as much sugar as you need. If you cannot find palm sugar, soft brown sugar is a fairly good substitute.

### Jasmine flowers

These pretty, delicate white flowers have a light, floral fragrance and are often infused in syrup and used to flavour desserts and cakes. The flowers are available only in season. Jasmine essence can be used as a substitute but it lacks the subtlety imparted by the fresh flowers.

### SPICE PASTES

There are many classic Thai curry pastes, all with their own individual blends of herbs and spices. Green, red and yellow curry pastes are used to make hot curries with plenty of liquid. Very good ready-made versions are available in most supermarkets.

### Green curry paste

This hot and spicy paste is a blend of chillies, aromatics and plenty of fresh herbs, giving the finished paste a greenish colour. It is most often used to make chicken and vegetable curries.

### Red curry paste

Made with plenty of fresh red chillies, this fiery, red-brown paste is a complex blend of aromatics and spices. It is most frequently used in beef and chicken curries.

### Yellow curry paste

This golden brown paste is very spicy. It contains fresh turmeric and is usually used in chicken and beef curries.

### Magic paste

This fragrant paste made from crushed garlic, white pepper and coriander (cilantro) is often used to flavour soups and curries. It is available from Thai and Asian stores.

*Below: Good quality yellow curry paste can be bought ready-made from Asian stores and some large supermarkets.*

## SAUCES

There are a number of essential sauces used for flavouring Thai dishes. Some are also used as a condiment.

### Fish sauce

*Nam pla* is one of the most important ingredients used in the Thai kitchen. Made from fermented salted fish, the clear orange-brown sauce has a very salty, pungent aroma and flavour that mellows during cooking. It is available from Asian stores.

### Soy sauce

Two types of soy sauce are used in Thai cooking: salty and sweet. There are light and dark varieties of both salty and sweet sauces. They are most frequently used in stir-fries, sauces and dressings. Soy sauce can vary greatly in quality, so buy a reputable brand. Store it in the refrigerator once opened.

### Chilli sauce

This thick, dark red sauce is very fiery and is used for flavouring and as a condiment. Use with caution because it is very strong. It is available from most supermarkets and Asian stores.

### Shrimp paste

Also known as blachan or terasi, this dark brown paste is a key flavouring in Thai cooking. Made from fermented, salted and dried pulverized shrimp, it has a very pungent flavour and is usually heated before adding to a dish to help mellow the flavour. It is available from Asian stores in compressed blocks, cans or tubs.

### Dried shrimp

These tiny, salty shellfish have a strong flavour and are used as a flavouring in salads and other dishes. They are available in Asian stores, and are usually found in plastic bags in the chiller or freezer cabinets. Choose shrimp with a pinkish colour, and avoid any with a greyish tinge.

*Above: Piquant sweet chilli sauce is used both as a flavouring and as a spicy dipping sauce.*

### Sweet chilli sauce

This thick translucent orange sauce is specked with red chilli. It has a much more delicate, fruitier flavour than chilli sauce and may be used as a flavouring ingredient or dipping sauce. It is available from supermarkets and Asian stores.

### Black bean sauce

This pungent mixture of puréed black beans, soy sauce, sugar and spices is used to add an earthy flavour to many savoury dishes. It is available from Asian stores and some supermarkets.

### Oyster sauce

This thick, dark brown sauce originated in China but is popular in Thai cooking. Based on soy sauce and oyster extract, it has a distinctive salty, slightly sweet taste and is used as a flavouring in many dishes. It is best added towards the end of cooking time. It is available from Asian stores and supermarkets. A vegetarian version made from mushrooms is also available.

### Plum sauce

This tangy, spicy sweet-and-sour sauce also originated in China. It is used as a flavouring ingredient and also as a dipping sauce. It is widely available in large supermarkets and Asian stores.

## RICE

In Thailand, rice is considered the most important ingredient: the average Thai consumes about 158kg/350lb rice a year. There are two main types: jasmine (or Thai) fragrant rice and glutinous rice. Jasmine rice has long grains and a scented flavour. Once cooked, the translucent grains become white and fluffy. Glutinous rice, also known as sweet or sticky rice, may have short, round grains or long grains. When cooked, they clump together, allowing the rice to be rolled into balls and eaten with the hands. Rice flour, made from ground rice, is also widely used – in noodles, pancakes and desserts.

### Cooking jasmine rice

The amount of water needed will vary slightly depending on variety, but as a general guide, use about 600ml/1 pint/2½ cups water for 225g/8oz/generous 1 cup rice.

**1** Put the rice in a large bowl and pour over cold water to cover. Gently swirl the grains until the water turns cloudy. Leave to settle, then drain. Repeat several times until the water runs clear.

**2** Put the rice in a pan and pour in the measured water. Bring to the boil, then reduce the heat to very low. Cover tightly and cook until all the liquid has been absorbed (up to 25 minutes).

**3** Remove the pan from the heat and leave, covered, in a warm place for 5 minutes until tender.

*Above: Fresh egg noodles usually come packed in nests, and are available from Chinese and Asian supermarkets.*

## NOODLES

Different types of noodles are used either as an ingredient or an accompaniment. Rice noodles are made from rice flour and come in several widths: very thin vermicelli rice noodles, medium rice noodles, which resemble spaghetti, and rice stick noodles, which are flat, rather like tagliatelle. All are available dried; rice stick noodles are also available fresh. Rice noodles do not need to be boiled, they can simply be soaked in boiling water for a few minutes until soft. Fresh noodles are sticky so should be separated before soaking.

Yellow egg noodles are made with wheat flour. They are available fresh or dried and come in various shapes: round ones for stir-frying and flat ones for soups. Egg noodles need to be cooked in boiling water for 4 minutes, or according to the packet instructions.

Transparent cellophane noodles, also known as glass or bean thread noodles, are very thin and wiry. Available dried, they are always used as an ingredient. To prepare, soak in boiling water.

## FISH AND SHELLFISH

Thailand has long coastlines and many rivers, which offer an abundant supply of fish and shellfish, including prawns (shrimp), crab, squid, and many types of fish. They are used in many dishes.

## POULTRY AND MEAT

Chicken is used in many Thai dishes, including salads, soups, stir-fries and curries. Duck and guinea fowl are also popular. Pork is widely eaten throughout South-east Asia, and beef is also used.

## TOFU

Also known as beancurd, tofu is made from fermented soya beans. There are two types of fresh tofu: silken and firm. Silken tofu is very soft and is often used in soups, while firm tofu can withstand more rigorous handling. Both are a creamy white colour, and are sold in blocks. Deep-fried tofu is golden brown and chewy and is used in soups, salads, stir-fries and curries.

## VEGETABLES

As well as the many vegetables such as carrots, broccoli and beansprouts that are commonly found in the West, there are some more unusual ones that are widely used in the Thai kitchen. They can be found in specialist Asian stores and some larger supermarkets.

### Shallots

Thai shallots have a pinkish tinge and are smaller and more pungent than those seen in the West. They are used in a wide variety of dishes, while deep-fried shallots are used as a garnish.

*Below: Thai shallots are an essential ingredient, and are used in spice pastes, soups, stir-fries and curries.*

### Salted eggs

These preserved duck eggs are served as an accompaniment. They are very salty, so one egg will serve several people. They are available from Asian stores and will keep for about 1 month.

### Chinese leaves/Chinese cabbage

This mild, sweet vegetable has long, crinkled pale green leaves with a crunchy white central rib. It is widely available and is used in salads, soups and stir-fries. It can be stored in the refrigerator for several weeks.

### Chinese broccoli

Similar to purple sprouting broccoli, this vegetable has long slender stems, loose leaves and a cluster of tiny white flowers at its centre. It has a peppery, cabbage-like flavour and may be served on its own as a side dish or added to soups, stir-fries and curries. Use quickly because it deteriorates.

### Morning glory

Also known as water convolvulus or water spinach, this leafy vegetable has long, narrow green leaves with slender stems. It tastes rather like spinach. It does not keep well, so use as soon as possible after purchase.

### Pak choi/Bok choy

This member of the cabbage family has broad white stems topped with lush dark green leaves. It has a slightly peppery flavour and may be eaten raw, or cooked in soups and stir-fries. Store in the refrigerator for 2–3 days.

### Mushrooms

Many different types of mushroom are used in Thai salads, soups, stir-fries and curries. Button (white), chestnut, oyster and shiitake mushrooms are available fresh and can be stored in a paper bag in the refrigerator for a few days. Shiitake mushrooms are also available dried and should be soaked in boiling water before use. Tiny straw mushrooms are available in cans.

### Aubergine/Eggplant

Several different types of aubergine are used in Thailand: long aubergines, small round apple aubergines and tiny pea aubergines. Depending on variety, they vary from white to pale green and purple. They are used in many different dishes, including curries and stir-fries.

### Bamboo shoots

These creamy white shoots have a crisp texture and mild flavour and are used in salads, soups, stir-fries and curries. They are available canned and should be drained and rinsed well before use.

### Mooli/Daikon

This long white root has a crisp, juicy texture and mild, peppery flavour rather like radish. It may be grated in salads or added to soups, stir-fries and curries. It should be peeled before use.

### Snake beans/Yard long beans

Also known as asparagus beans or Thai beans, these resemble exceptionally long green beans – with many growing up to 40cm/16in. They may be pale or dark green; the latter are tastier. Try to choose young, narrow beans with underdeveloped seeds because older beans tend to be tough. Store in the refrigerator and use within 3 days of purchase, before they turn yellow.

*Below: Morning glory is a very popular vegetable in Thailand. It is eaten raw, or cooked in soups and stir-fries.*

*Above: When buying rambutans, look out for brightly coloured fruits with green-tipped hairs.*

### FRUIT

As well as common tropical fruits such as mangoes and lychees, Thai cooks use many other, more unusual fruits that are available from Asian stores.

### Asian pear

These round pears have a golden-brown skin and crisp, juicy white flesh. They are good eaten raw, but are also used in savoury salads. Store in the refrigerator.

### Papaya

Also known as a paw-paw, this sweet, scented fruit has meltingly tender flesh surrounding a clutch of shiny black seeds. To prepare the ripe fruit, halve and scoop out the seeds. Choose unblemished ripe fruit that is orange all over or, if you do not plan to use it immediately, choose slightly firm fruit with a greenish skin that is turning orange. Ripe papayas will keep in the refrigerator for about a week. Unripe, or green, papaya is used as a vegetable in salads, soups and curries.

### Pitaya/Dragon fruit

These stunning bright pink or yellow fruits have green-tipped scales. Inside, the flesh is white, specked with tiny black, edible seeds. It has a crisp texture and mild flavour. Ripe fruit should yield slightly when squeezed.

### Pomelo

There are several varieties of this very large, round citrus fruit. The fruits may have a greenish-yellow rind and creamy white flesh, or dark green rind and sweet, juicy, pink flesh. The fruit may be eaten on its own or used in salads. Whole, unpeeled fruits will keep at room temperature for about 1 month.

### Rambutan

This "hairy" red-skinned fruit has a translucent white flesh with a sweet, scented flavour like lychee surrounding a large stone (pit). They can be stored in the refrigerator for up to 1 week.

### NUTS AND SEEDS

Many different nuts and seeds are used in Thai cooking. Peanuts are often crushed and added to sauces and spicy curries, while cashew nuts may be used whole. Sesame seeds add a wonderful rich flavour to many dishes including salads, stir-fries and curries.

### Banana flower

Also called banana blossom or banana bud, this is actually the unopened heart of the banana flower. It has a mild taste and tender texture rather like an artichoke heart, and is used in salads and soups. Banana flowers are available fresh, canned or dried. Once cut, the fresh flower discolours, so brush with lemon juice to prevent it turning brown.

# SOUPS AND APPETIZERS

In Thai city streets vendors with portable carts cook enticing snacks using ingredients such as garlic, ginger, chillies and vegetables. Snacks also make great appetizers, so start your meal with delicious but easy-to-make dishes such as Roasted Coconut Cashew Nuts or Corn Fritters. Soups may be served solo, as a light lunch, as a first course or Thai-style as part of a multi-dish meal. Authentic Thai treats such as Pumpkin and Coconut Soup and Northern Squash Soup are certain to be popular.

# ROASTED COCONUT CASHEW NUTS

*SERVE THESE HOT AND SWEET CASHEW NUTS IN PAPER OR CELLOPHANE CONES AT PARTIES. NOT ONLY DO THEY LOOK ENTICING AND TASTE TERRIFIC, BUT THE CONES HELP TO KEEP CLOTHES AND HANDS CLEAN AND CAN SIMPLY BE THROWN AWAY AFTERWARDS.*

**SERVES SIX TO EIGHT**

INGREDIENTS
   15ml/1 tbsp groundnut (peanut) oil
   30ml/2 tbsp clear honey
   250g/9oz/2 cups cashew nuts
   115g/4oz/1⅓ cups desiccated (dry
      unsweetened shredded) coconut
   2 small fresh red chillies, seeded and
      finely chopped
   salt and ground black pepper

**VARIATIONS**
Almonds also work well, or choose
peanuts for a more economical snack.

**1** Heat the oil in a wok or large frying pan and then stir in the honey. After a few seconds add the nuts and coconut and stir-fry until both are golden brown.

**2** Add the chillies, with salt and pepper to taste. Toss until all the ingredients are well mixed. Serve warm or cooled in paper cones or saucers.

# CORN FRITTERS

*SOMETIMES IT IS THE SIMPLEST DISHES THAT TASTE THE BEST. THESE FRITTERS, PACKED WITH CRUNCHY CORN, ARE VERY EASY TO PREPARE AND UNDERSTANDABLY POPULAR.*

MAKES TWELVE

INGREDIENTS

3 corn cobs, total weight about 250g/9oz
1 garlic clove, crushed
small bunch fresh coriander (cilantro), chopped
1 small fresh red or green chilli, seeded and finely chopped
1 spring onion (scallion), finely chopped
15ml/1 tbsp soy sauce
75g/3oz/¾ cup rice flour or plain (all-purpose) flour
2 eggs, lightly beaten
60ml/4 tbsp water
oil, for shallow frying
salt and ground black pepper
sweet chilli sauce, to serve

**1** Using a sharp knife, slice the kernels from the cobs and place them in a large bowl. Add the garlic, chopped coriander, red or green chilli, spring onion, soy sauce, flour, beaten eggs and water and mix well. Season with salt and pepper to taste and mix again. The mixture should be firm enough to hold its shape, but not stiff.

**2** Heat the oil in a large frying pan. Add spoonfuls of the corn mixture, gently spreading each one out with the back of the spoon to make a roundish fritter. Cook for 1–2 minutes on each side.

**3** Drain on kitchen paper and keep hot while frying more fritters in the same way. Serve hot with sweet chilli sauce.

# PRAWN AND SESAME TOASTS

*THESE ATTRACTIVE LITTLE TOAST TRIANGLES ARE IDEAL FOR SERVING WITH PRE-DINNER DRINKS AND ARE ALWAYS A FAVOURITE HOT SNACK AT PARTIES. THEY ARE SURPRISINGLY EASY TO PREPARE AND YOU CAN COOK THEM IN JUST A FEW MINUTES.*

SERVES FOUR

INGREDIENTS

225g/8oz peeled raw prawns (shrimp)
15ml/1 tbsp sherry
15ml/1 tbsp soy sauce
30ml/2 tbsp cornflour (cornstarch)
2 egg whites
4 slices white bread
115g/4oz/½ cup sesame seeds
oil, for deep-frying
sweet chilli sauce,
  to serve

1 Process the prawns, sherry, soy sauce and cornflour in a food processor.

2 In a grease-free bowl, whisk the egg whites until stiff. Fold them into the prawn and cornflour mixture.

3 Cut each slice of bread into four triangular quarters. Spread out the sesame seeds on a large plate. Spread the prawn paste over one side of each bread triangle, then press the coated sides into the sesame seeds so that they stick and cover the prawn paste.

4 Heat the oil in a wok or deep-fryer, to 190°C/375°F or until a cube of bread, added to the oil, browns in about 45 seconds. Add the toasts, a few at a time, prawn side down, and deep-fry for 2–3 minutes, then turn and fry on the other side until golden.

5 Drain on kitchen paper and serve hot with sweet chilli sauce.

# RICE CAKES <u>WITH</u> SPICY DIPPING SAUCE

*A CLASSIC THAI APPETIZER, THESE RICE CAKES ARE EASY TO MAKE AND WILL KEEP ALMOST
INDEFINITELY IN AN AIRTIGHT CONTAINER. START MAKING THEM AT LEAST A DAY BEFORE YOU
PLAN TO SERVE THEM, AS THE RICE NEEDS TO DRY OUT OVERNIGHT.*

SERVES FOUR TO SIX

INGREDIENTS
175g/6oz/1 cup Thai jasmine rice
350ml/12fl oz/1½ cups water
oil, for deep-frying and greasing
For the spicy dipping sauce
6–8 dried chillies
2.5ml/½ tsp salt
2 shallots, chopped
2 garlic cloves, chopped
4 coriander (cilantro) roots
10 white peppercorns
250ml/8fl oz/1 cup coconut milk
5ml/1 tsp shrimp paste
115g/4oz minced (ground) pork
115g/4oz cherry tomatoes, chopped
15ml/1 tbsp Thai fish sauce
15ml/1 tbsp palm sugar or light
    muscovado (brown) sugar
30ml/2 tbsp tamarind juice (tamarind
    paste mixed with warm water)
30ml/2 tbsp coarsely chopped
    roasted peanuts
2 spring onions (scallions), chopped

**1** Make the sauce. Snap off the stems of the chillies, shake out the seeds and soak the chillies in warm water for 20 minutes. Drain and put in a mortar. Sprinkle over the salt and crush. Add the shallots, garlic, coriander and peppercorns. Pound to a coarse paste.

**2** Pour the coconut milk into a pan and bring to the boil. When it begins to separate, stir in the pounded chilli paste. Cook for 2–3 minutes, until the mixture is fragrant. Stir in the shrimp paste and cook for 1 minute more.

**3** Add the pork, stirring to break up any lumps. Cook for 5–10 minutes, then stir in the tomatoes, fish sauce, palm sugar and tamarind juice. Simmer, stirring occasionally, until the sauce thickens, then stir in the chopped peanuts and spring onions. Remove the sauce from the heat and leave to cool.

**4** Preheat the oven to the lowest setting. Grease a baking sheet. Wash the rice in several changes of water. Put it in a pan, add the water and cover tightly. Bring to the boil, reduce the heat and simmer gently for about 15 minutes.

**5** Remove the lid and fluff up the rice. Spoon it on to the baking sheet and press it down with the back of a spoon. Leave in the oven to dry out overnight.

**6** Break the rice into bitesize pieces. Heat the oil in a wok or deep-fryer. Deep-fry the rice cakes, in batches, for about 1 minute, until they puff up but are not browned. Remove and drain well. Serve with the dipping sauce.

# EGG ROLLS

*THE TITLE OF THIS RECIPE COULD LEAD TO SOME CONFUSION, ESPECIALLY IN THE UNITED STATES, WHERE EGG ROLLS ARE THE SAME AS SPRING ROLLS. THESE EGG ROLLS, HOWEVER, ARE WEDGES OF A ROLLED THAI-FLAVOURED OMELETTE. THEY ARE FREQUENTLY SERVED AS FINGER FOOD.*

SERVES TWO

INGREDIENTS
   3 eggs, beaten
   15ml/1 tbsp soy sauce
   1 bunch garlic chives, thinly sliced
   1–2 small fresh red or green chillies,
      seeded and finely chopped
   small bunch fresh coriander
      (cilantro), chopped
   pinch of granulated sugar
   salt and ground black pepper
   15ml/1 tbsp groundnut (peanut) oil
For the dipping sauce
   60ml/4 tbsp light soy sauce
   fresh lime juice, to taste

**COOK'S TIP**
Wear gloves while preparing chillies or cut them up with a knife and fork. Wash your hands after in warm, soapy water.

**1** Make the dipping sauce. Pour the soy sauce into a bowl. Add a generous squeeze of lime juice. Taste and add more lime juice if needed.

**2** Mix the eggs, soy sauce, chives, chillies and coriander. Add the sugar and season to taste. Heat the oil in a large frying pan, pour in the egg mixture and swirl the pan to make an omelette.

**3** Cook for 1–2 minutes, until the omelette is just firm and the underside is golden. Slide it out on to a plate and roll up as though it were a pancake. Leave to cool completely.

**4** When the omelette is cool, slice it diagonally in 1cm/½in pieces. Arrange the slices on a serving platter and serve with the bowl of dipping sauce.

# SON-IN-LAW EGGS

*THE FASCINATING NAME FOR THIS DISH COMES FROM A STORY ABOUT A PROSPECTIVE BRIDEGROOM WHO VERY MUCH WANTED TO IMPRESS HIS FUTURE MOTHER-IN-LAW AND DEVISED A NEW RECIPE BASED ON THE ONLY DISH HE KNEW HOW TO MAKE — BOILED EGGS.*

SERVES FOUR TO SIX

INGREDIENTS
    30ml/2 tbsp vegetable oil
    6 shallots, thinly sliced
    6 garlic cloves, thinly sliced
    6 fresh red chillies, sliced
    oil, for deep-frying
    6 hard-boiled eggs, shelled
    salad leaves, to serve
    sprigs of fresh coriander (cilantro),
      to garnish (optional)
For the sauce
    75g/3oz/6 tbsp palm sugar or light
      muscovado (brown) sugar
    75ml/5 tbsp Thai fish sauce
    90ml/6 tbsp tamarind juice

**COOK'S TIP**
The level of heat varies, depending on which type of chillies are used and whether you include the seeds.

**1** Make the sauce. Put the sugar, fish sauce and tamarind juice in a pan. Bring to the boil, stirring until the sugar dissolves, lower the heat and simmer for 5 minutes. Taste and add more sugar, fish sauce or tamarind juice, if needed. Transfer the sauce to a bowl.

**2** Heat the vegetable oil in a frying pan and cook the shallots, garlic and chillies for 5 minutes. Transfer to a bowl.

**3** Heat the oil in a deep-fryer or wok to 190°C/375°F or until a cube of day-old bread, added to the oil, browns in about 45 seconds. Deep-fry the eggs in the hot oil for 3–5 minutes, until golden brown. Remove from the oil and drain well on kitchen paper. Cut the eggs into quarters and arrange them on a bed of salad leaves. Drizzle with the sauce, sprinkle over the shallot mixture and serve immediately.

# HOT AND SWEET VEGETABLE AND TOFU SOUP

*AN INTERESTING COMBINATION OF HOT, SWEET AND SOUR FLAVOURS THAT MAKES FOR A SOOTHING, NUTRITIOUS SOUP. IT TAKES ONLY MINUTES TO MAKE AS THE SPINACH AND SILKEN TOFU ARE SIMPLY PLACED IN BOWLS AND COVERED WITH THE FLAVOURED HOT STOCK.*

SERVES FOUR

INGREDIENTS
  1.2 litres/2 pints/5 cups
    vegetable stock
  5–10ml/1–2 tsp Thai red
    curry paste
  2 kaffir lime leaves, torn
  40g/1½oz/3 tbsp palm sugar or light
    muscovado (brown) sugar
  30ml/2 tbsp soy sauce
  juice of 1 lime
  1 carrot, cut into thin batons
  50g/2oz baby spinach leaves, any
    coarse stalks removed
  225g/8oz block silken tofu, diced

**1** Heat the stock in a large pan, then add the red curry paste. Stir constantly over a medium heat until the paste has dissolved. Add the lime leaves, sugar and soy sauce and bring to the boil.

**2** Add the lime juice and carrot to the pan. Reduce the heat and simmer for 5–10 minutes. Place the spinach and tofu in four individual serving bowls and pour the hot stock on top to serve.

# MIXED VEGETABLE SOUP

*IN THAILAND, THIS TYPE OF SOUP IS USUALLY MADE IN LARGE QUANTITIES AND THEN REHEATED FOR CONSUMPTION OVER SEVERAL DAYS. IF YOU WOULD LIKE TO DO THE SAME, DOUBLE OR TREBLE THE QUANTITIES. CHILL LEFTOVER SOUP RAPIDLY AND REHEAT THOROUGHLY BEFORE SERVING.*

### SERVES FOUR

INGREDIENTS
    30ml/2 tbsp groundnut (peanut) oil
    15ml/1 tbsp magic paste (see
      Cook's Tip)
    90g/3½oz Savoy cabbage or
      Chinese leaves (Chinese cabbage),
      finely shredded
    90g/3½oz mooli (daikon),
      finely diced
    1 medium cauliflower,
      coarsely chopped
    4 celery sticks, coarsely chopped
    1.2 litres/2 pints/5 cups
      vegetable stock
    130g/4½oz fried tofu, cut into
      2.5cm/1in cubes
    5ml/1 tsp palm sugar or light
      muscovado (brown) sugar
    45ml/3 tbsp light soy sauce

**1** Heat the groundnut oil in a large, heavy pan or wok. Add the magic paste and cook over a low heat, stirring frequently, until it gives off its aroma. Add the shredded Savoy cabbage or Chinese leaves, mooli, cauliflower and celery. Pour in the vegetable stock, increase the heat to medium and bring to the boil, stirring occasionally. Gently stir in the tofu cubes.

**2** Add the sugar and soy sauce. Reduce the heat and simmer for 15 minutes, until the vegetables are cooked and tender. Taste and add a little more soy sauce if needed. Serve hot.

**COOK'S TIP**
Magic paste is a mixture of crushed garlic, white pepper and coriander (cilantro). Look for it at Thai markets.

# OMELETTE SOUP

*A VERY SATISFYING SOUP THAT IS QUICK AND EASY TO PREPARE. IT IS VERSATILE, TOO, IN THAT YOU CAN VARY THE VEGETABLES ACCORDING TO WHAT IS AVAILABLE.*

SERVES FOUR

INGREDIENTS

  1 egg
  15ml/1 tbsp groundnut (peanut) oil
  900ml/1½ pints/3¾ cups
    vegetable stock
  2 large carrots, finely diced
  4 outer leaves Savoy
    cabbage, shredded
  30ml/2 tbsp soy sauce
  2.5ml/½ tsp granulated sugar
  2.5ml/½ tsp ground black pepper
  fresh coriander (cilantro) leaves,
    to garnish

**VARIATION**

Use pak choi (bok choy) instead of Savoy cabbage. In Thailand there are about forty different types of pak choi, including miniature versions.

**1** Put the egg in a bowl and beat lightly with a fork. Heat the oil in a small frying pan until it is hot, but not smoking. Pour in the egg and swirl the pan so that it coats the base evenly. Cook over a medium heat until the omelette has set and the underside is golden. Slide it out of the pan and roll it up like a pancake. Slice into 5mm/¼in rounds and set aside for the garnish.

**2** Put the stock into a large pan. Add the carrots and cabbage and bring to the boil. Reduce the heat and simmer for 5 minutes, then add the soy sauce, granulated sugar and pepper.

**3** Stir well, then pour into warmed bowls. Lay a few omelette rounds on the surface of each portion and complete the garnish with the coriander leaves.

# NORTHERN SQUASH SOUP

*AS THE TITLE OF THE RECIPE SUGGESTS, THIS COMES FROM NORTHERN THAILAND. IT IS QUITE HEARTY, SOMETHING OF A CROSS BETWEEN A SOUP AND A STEW. THE BANANA FLOWER ISN'T ESSENTIAL, BUT IT DOES ADD A UNIQUE AND AUTHENTIC FLAVOUR.*

SERVES FOUR

INGREDIENTS

1 butternut squash, about 300g/11oz
1 litre/1¾ pints/4 cups
  vegetable stock
90g/3½ oz/scant 1 cup green beans,
  cut into 2.5cm/1in pieces
45g/1¾ oz dried banana
  flower (optional)
15ml/1 tbsp Thai fish sauce
225g/8oz raw prawns (shrimp)
small bunch fresh basil
cooked rice, to serve
For the chilli paste
115g/4oz shallots, sliced
10 drained bottled green peppercorns
1 small fresh green chilli, seeded and
  finely chopped
2.5ml/½ tsp shrimp paste

**1** Peel the butternut squash and cut it in half. Scoop out the seeds with a teaspoon and discard, then cut the flesh into neat cubes. Set aside.

**2** Make the chilli paste by pounding the shallots, peppercorns, chilli and shrimp paste together using a mortar and pestle or puréeing them in a spice blender.

**3** Heat the stock gently in a large pan, then stir in the chilli paste. Add the squash, beans and banana flower, if using. Bring to the boil and cook for 15 minutes.

**4** Add the fish sauce, prawns and basil. Bring to simmering point, then simmer for 3 minutes. Serve in warmed bowls, accompanied by rice.

# PUMPKIN AND COCONUT SOUP

*THE NATURAL SWEETNESS OF THE PUMPKIN IS HEIGHTENED BY THE ADDITION OF A LITTLE SUGAR IN THIS LOVELY LOOKING SOUP, BUT THIS IS BALANCED BY THE CHILLIES, SHRIMP PASTE AND DRIED SHRIMP. COCONUT CREAM BLURS THE BOUNDARIES BEAUTIFULLY.*

SERVES FOUR TO SIX

INGREDIENTS
    450g/1lb pumpkin
    2 garlic cloves, crushed
    4 shallots, finely chopped
    2.5ml/½ tsp shrimp paste
    1 lemon grass stalk, chopped
    2 fresh green chillies, seeded
    15ml/1 tbsp dried shrimp soaked
        for 10 minutes in warm water
        to cover
    600ml/1 pint/2½ cups
        chicken stock
    600ml/1 pint/2½ cups
        coconut cream
    30ml/2 tbsp Thai fish sauce
    5ml/1 tsp granulated sugar
    115g/4oz small cooked shelled
        prawns (shrimp)
    salt and ground black pepper
To garnish
    2 fresh red chillies, seeded and
        thinly sliced
    10–12 fresh basil leaves

**1** Peel the pumpkin and cut it into quarters with a sharp knife. Scoop out the seeds with a teaspoon and discard. Cut the flesh into chunks about 2cm/¾in thick and set aside.

**2** Put the garlic, shallots, shrimp paste, lemon grass, green chillies and salt to taste in a mortar. Drain the dried shrimp, discarding the soaking liquid, and add them, then use a pestle to grind the mixture into a paste. Alternatively, place all the ingredients in a food processor and process to a paste.

**3** Bring the chicken stock to the boil in a large pan. Add the ground paste and stir well to dissolve.

**4** Add the pumpkin chunks and bring to a simmer. Simmer for 10–15 minutes, or until the pumpkin is tender.

**5** Stir in the coconut cream, then bring the soup back to simmering point. Do not let it boil. Add the fish sauce, sugar and ground black pepper to taste.

**6** Add the prawns and cook for a further 2–3 minutes, until they are heated through. Serve in warm soup bowls, garnished with chillies and basil leaves.

**COOK'S TIP**
Shrimp paste is made from ground shrimp fermented in brine.

# SMOKED MACKEREL AND TOMATO SOUP

*ALL THE INGREDIENTS FOR THIS UNUSUAL SOUP ARE COOKED IN A SINGLE PAN, SO IT IS NOT ONLY QUICK AND EASY TO PREPARE, BUT REDUCES THE CLEARING UP. SMOKED MACKEREL GIVES THE SOUP A ROBUST FLAVOUR, BUT THIS IS TEMPERED BY THE CITRUS TONES IN THE LEMON GRASS AND TAMARIND.*

SERVES FOUR

INGREDIENTS
    200g/7oz smoked mackerel fillets
    4 tomatoes
    1 litre/1¾ pints/4 cups
      vegetable stock
    1 lemon grass stalk, finely chopped
    5cm/2in piece fresh galangal,
      finely diced
    4 shallots, finely chopped
    2 garlic cloves, finely chopped
    2.5ml/½ tsp dried chilli flakes
    15ml/1 tbsp Thai fish sauce
    5ml/1 tsp palm sugar or light
      muscovado (brown) sugar
    45ml/3 tbsp thick tamarind juice,
      made by mixing tamarind paste with
      warm water
    small bunch fresh chives or spring
      onions (scallions), to garnish

**1** Prepare the smoked mackerel fillets. Remove and discard the skin, if necessary, then chop the flesh into large pieces. Remove any stray bones with your fingers or a pair of tweezers.

**2** Cut the tomatoes in half, squeeze out most of the seeds with your fingers, then finely dice the flesh with a sharp knife. Set aside.

**3** Pour the stock into a large pan and add the lemon grass, galangal, shallots and garlic. Bring to the boil, reduce the heat and simmer for 15 minutes.

**4** Add the fish, tomatoes, chilli flakes, fish sauce, sugar and tamarind juice. Simmer for 4–5 minutes, until the fish and tomatoes are heated through. Serve garnished with chives or spring onions.

# SALADS AND VEGETABLE DISHES

*Like all hot countries, Thailand has a fine repertoire of salads and cold dishes. These aren't salads in the Western sense, but rather combinations of fresh and cooked vegetables, often with noodles or fruit such as papaya or mango. This chapter contains a selection of salads and nutritious vegetable dishes that can be eaten alone or served with a main dish. Their crisp textures and aromatic flavours provides a refreshing complement and perfect balance to the curries and main dishes in this book.*

# BAMBOO SHOOT SALAD

*THIS HOT, SHARP-FLAVOURED SALAD ORIGINATED IN NORTH-EASTERN THAILAND. USE CANNED WHOLE BAMBOO SHOOTS, IF YOU CAN FIND THEM — THEY HAVE MORE FLAVOUR THAN SLICED ONES.*

### SERVES FOUR

INGREDIENTS

    400g/14oz canned bamboo shoots, in
      large pieces
    25g/1oz/about 3 tbsp glutinous rice
    30ml/2 tbsp chopped shallots
    15ml/1 tbsp chopped garlic
    45ml/3 tbsp chopped spring
      onions (scallions)
    30ml/2 tbsp Thai fish sauce
    30ml/2 tbsp fresh lime juice
    5ml/1 tsp granulated sugar
    2.5ml/½ tsp dried chilli flakes
    20–25 small fresh mint leaves
    15ml/1 tbsp toasted sesame seeds

**COOK'S TIP**
Glutinous rice does not, in fact, contain any gluten – it's just sticky.

**1** Rinse the bamboo shoots under cold running water, then drain them and pat them thoroughly dry with kitchen paper and set them aside.

**2** Dry-roast the rice in a frying pan until it is golden brown. Leave to cool slightly, then tip into a mortar and grind to fine crumbs with a pestle.

**3** Transfer the rice to a bowl and add the shallots, garlic, spring onions, fish sauce, lime juice, sugar, chillies and half the mint leaves. Mix well.

**4** Add the bamboo shoots to the bowl and toss to mix. Serve sprinkled with the toasted sesame seeds and the remaining mint leaves.

# CABBAGE SALAD

*THIS IS A SIMPLE AND DELICIOUS WAY OF SERVING A SOMEWHAT MUNDANE VEGETABLE. CLASSIC THAI FLAVOURS PERMEATE THIS COLOURFUL WARM SALAD.*

SERVES FOUR TO SIX

INGREDIENTS
  30ml/2 tbsp vegetable oil
  2 large fresh red chillies, seeded and
    cut into thin strips
  6 garlic cloves, thinly sliced
  6 shallots, thinly sliced
  1 small cabbage, shredded
  30ml/2 tbsp coarsely chopped
    roasted peanuts, to garnish
For the dressing
  30ml/2 tbsp Thai fish sauce
  grated rind of 1 lime
  30ml/2 tbsp fresh lime juice
  120ml/4fl oz/½ cup coconut milk

**VARIATION**
Other vegetables, such as cauliflower, broccoli and Chinese leaves (Chinese cabbage), can be cooked in this way.

**1** Make the dressing by mixing the fish sauce, lime rind and juice and coconut milk in a bowl. Whisk until thoroughly combined, then set aside.

**2** Heat the oil in a wok. Stir-fry the chillies, garlic and shallots over a medium heat for 3–4 minutes, until the shallots are brown and crisp. Remove with a slotted spoon and set aside.

**3** Bring a large pan of lightly salted water to the boil. Add the cabbage and blanch for 2–3 minutes. Place it in a colander, drain well and put into a bowl.

**4** Whisk the dressing again, add it to the warm cabbage and toss to mix. Transfer the salad to a serving dish. Sprinkle with the fried shallot mixture and the peanuts. Serve immediately.

# RAW VEGETABLE YAM

*IN THIS CONTEXT, THE WORD "YAM" DOES NOT REFER TO THE STARCHY VEGETABLE THAT RESEMBLES SWEET POTATO, BUT RATHER TO A UNIQUE STYLE OF THAI COOKING. YAM DISHES ARE SALADS MADE WITH RAW OR LIGHTLY COOKED VEGETABLES, DRESSED WITH A SPECIAL SPICY SAUCE.*

SERVES FOUR

INGREDIENTS
   50g/2oz watercress or baby
     spinach, chopped
   ½ cucumber, finely diced
   2 celery sticks, finely diced
   2 carrots, finely diced
   1 red (bell) pepper, seeded and
     finely diced
   2 tomatoes, seeded and
     finely diced
   small bunch fresh mint, chopped
   90g/3½oz cellophane noodles
For the yam
   2 small fresh red chillies, seeded
     and finely chopped
   60ml/4 tbsp light soy sauce
   45ml/3 tbsp lemon juice
   5ml/1 tsp palm sugar or light
     muscovado (brown) sugar
   60ml/4 tbsp water
   1 head pickled garlic, finely
     chopped, plus 15ml/1 tbsp vinegar
     from the jar
   50g/2oz/scant ½ cup peanuts,
     roasted and chopped
   90g/3½oz fried tofu, finely chopped
   15ml/1 tbsp sesame seeds, toasted

**1** Place the watercress or spinach, cucumber, celery, carrots, red pepper and tomatoes in a bowl. Add the chopped mint and toss together.

**2** Soak the noodles in boiling water for 3 minutes, or according to the packet instructions, then drain well and snip with scissors into shorter lengths. Add them to the vegetables.

**3** Make the yam. Put the chopped chillies in a pan and add the soy sauce, lemon juice, sugar and water. Place over a medium heat and stir until the sugar has dissolved. Add the garlic, with the pickling vinegar from the jar, then mix in the chopped nuts, tofu and toasted sesame seeds.

**4** Pour the yam over the vegetables and noodles, toss together until well mixed, and serve immediately.

**VARIATIONS**
Any salad vegetables could be used for this recipe. Instead of dicing them, you could cut them into thin batons, preferably using a mandolin. The Thais like all the vegetable components in a dish like this to be of a small and uniform size so that all the different flavours and textures are experienced in a single mouthful.

# THAI FRUIT AND VEGETABLE SALAD

*THIS FRUIT SALAD IS TRADITIONALLY PRESENTED WITH THE MAIN COURSE AND SERVES AS A COOLER TO COUNTERACT THE HEAT OF THE CHILLIES THAT WILL INEVITABLY BE PRESENT IN THE OTHER DISHES. IT IS A TYPICALLY HARMONIOUS BALANCE OF FLAVOURS.*

SERVES FOUR TO SIX

INGREDIENTS

   1 small pineapple
   1 small mango, peeled and sliced
   1 green apple, cored and sliced
   6 rambutans or lychees, peeled and
     stoned (pitted)
   115g/4oz/1 cup green beans,
     trimmed and halved
   1 red onion, sliced
   1 small cucumber, cut into
     short sticks
   115g/4oz/1⅓ cups beansprouts
   2 spring onions (scallions), sliced
   1 ripe tomato, quartered
   225g/8oz cos, romaine or iceberg
     lettuce leaves
For the coconut dipping sauce
   30ml/2 tbsp coconut cream
   30ml/2 tbsp granulated sugar
   75ml/5 tbsp boiling water
   1.5ml/¼ tsp chilli sauce
   15ml/1 tbsp Thai fish sauce
   juice of 1 lime

**1** Make the coconut dipping sauce. Spoon the coconut cream, sugar and boiling water into a screw-top jar. Add the chilli and fish sauces and lime juice, close tightly and shake to mix.

**2** Trim both ends of the pineapple with a serrated knife, then cut away the outer skin. Remove the central core with an apple corer. Alternatively, quarter the pineapple lengthways and remove the portion of core from each wedge with a knife. Chop the pineapple and set aside with the other fruits.

**3** Bring a small pan of lightly salted water to the boil over a medium heat. Add the green beans and cook for 3–4 minutes, until just tender but still retaining some "bite". Drain, refresh under cold running water, drain well again and set aside.

**4** To serve, arrange all the fruits and vegetables in small heaps on a platter or in a shallow bowl. Pour the coconut sauce into a small serving bowl and serve separately as a dip.

# POMELO SALAD

*TYPICALLY, A THAI MEAL INCLUDES A SELECTION OF ABOUT FIVE DISHES, ONE OF WHICH IS OFTEN A REFRESHING AND PALATE-CLEANSING SALAD THAT FEATURES TROPICAL FRUIT.*

SERVES FOUR TO SIX

INGREDIENTS
   30ml/2 tbsp vegetable oil
   4 shallots, finely sliced
   2 garlic cloves, finely sliced
   1 large pomelo
   15ml/1 tbsp roasted peanuts
   115g/4oz cooked peeled
      prawns (shrimp)
   115g/4oz cooked crab meat
   10–12 small fresh mint leaves
For the dressing
   30ml/2 tbsp Thai fish sauce
   15ml/1 tbsp palm sugar or light
      muscovado (brown) sugar
   30ml/2 tbsp fresh lime juice
For the garnish
   2 spring onions (scallions),
      thinly sliced
   2 fresh red chillies, seeded and
      thinly sliced
   fresh coriander (cilantro) leaves
   shredded fresh coconut (optional)

**1** Make the dressing. Mix the fish sauce, sugar and lime juice in a bowl. Whisk well, then cover with clear film (plastic wrap) and set aside.

**2** Heat the oil in a small frying pan, add the shallots and garlic and cook over a medium heat until they are golden. Remove from the pan and set aside.

**3** Peel the pomelo and break the flesh into small pieces, taking care to remove any membranes.

**4** Grind the peanuts coarsely and put them in a salad bowl. Add the pomelo flesh, prawns, crab meat, mint leaves and the shallot mixture. Pour over the dressing, toss lightly and sprinkle with the spring onions, chillies and coriander leaves. Add the shredded coconut, if using. Serve immediately.

**COOK'S TIP**
The pomelo is a large citrus fruit that looks rather like a grapefruit, although it is not, as is sometimes thought, a hybrid. It is slightly pear-shaped with thick, yellow, dimpled skin and pinkish-yellow flesh that is both sturdier and drier than that of a grapefruit. It also has a sharper taste. Pomelos are sometimes known as "shaddocks" after the sea captain who brought them from their native Polynesia to the Caribbean.

# HOT AND SOUR NOODLE SALAD

*NOODLES MAKE THE PERFECT BASIS FOR A SALAD, ABSORBING THE DRESSING AND PROVIDING A*
*CONTRAST IN TEXTURE TO THE CRISP VEGETABLES.*

SERVES TWO

INGREDIENTS

   200g/7oz thin rice noodles
   small bunch fresh coriander (cilantro)
   2 tomatoes, seeded and sliced
   130g/4½oz baby corn cobs, sliced
   4 spring onions (scallions),
     thinly sliced
   1 red (bell) pepper, seeded and
     finely chopped
   juice of 2 limes
   2 small fresh green chillies, seeded
     and finely chopped
   10ml/2 tsp granulated sugar
   115g/4oz/1 cup peanuts, toasted
     and chopped
   30ml/2 tbsp soy sauce
   salt

**1** Bring a large pan of lightly salted water to the boil. Snap the noodles into short lengths, add to the pan and cook for 3–4 minutes. Drain, then rinse under cold water and drain again.

**2** Set aside a few coriander leaves for the garnish. Chop the remaining leaves and place them in a large serving bowl.

**3** Add the noodles to the bowl, with the tomato slices, corn cobs, spring onions, red pepper, lime juice, chillies, sugar and toasted peanuts. Season with the soy sauce, then taste and add a little salt if you think the mixture needs it. Toss the salad lightly but thoroughly, then garnish with the reserved coriander leaves and serve immediately.

# FRIED EGG SALAD

*CHILLIES AND EGGS MAY SEEM UNLIKELY PARTNERS, BUT ACTUALLY WORK VERY WELL TOGETHER. THE PEPPERY FLAVOUR OF THE WATERCRESS MAKES IT THE PERFECT FOUNDATION FOR THIS TASTY SALAD.*

### SERVES TWO

INGREDIENTS
15ml/1 tbsp groundnut (peanut) oil
1 garlic clove, thinly sliced
4 eggs
2 shallots, thinly sliced
2 small fresh red chillies, seeded and thinly sliced
½ small cucumber, finely diced
1cm/½in piece fresh root ginger, peeled and grated
juice of 2 limes
30ml/2 tbsp soy sauce
5ml/1 tsp caster (superfine) sugar
small bunch coriander (cilantro)
bunch watercress, coarsely chopped

**1** Heat the oil in a frying pan. Add the garlic and cook over a low heat until it starts to turn golden. Crack in the eggs. Break the yolks with a wooden spatula, then fry until the eggs are almost firm. Remove from the pan and set aside.

**2** Mix the shallots, chillies, cucumber and ginger in a bowl. In a separate bowl, whisk the lime juice with the soy sauce and sugar. Pour this dressing over the vegetables and toss lightly.

**3** Set aside a few coriander sprigs for the garnish. Chop the rest and add them to the salad. Toss it again.

**4** Reserve a few watercress sprigs and arrange the remainder on two serving plates. Cut the fried eggs into slices and divide them between the watercress mounds. Spoon the shallot mixture over them and serve, garnished with the reserved coriander and watercress.

# RICE SALAD

*THE SKY'S THE LIMIT WITH THIS RECIPE. USE WHATEVER FRUIT, VEGETABLES AND EVEN LEFTOVER MEAT THAT YOU MIGHT HAVE, MIX WITH COOKED RICE AND POUR OVER THE FRAGRANT DRESSING.*

SERVES FOUR TO SIX

INGREDIENTS
  350g/12oz/3 cups cooked rice
  1 Asian pear, cored and diced
  50g/2oz dried shrimp, chopped
  1 avocado, peeled, stoned (pitted)
    and diced
  ½ medium cucumber, finely diced
  2 lemon grass stalks, finely chopped
  30ml/2 tbsp sweet chilli sauce
  1 fresh green or red chilli, seeded
    and finely sliced
  115g/4oz/1 cup flaked (sliced)
    almonds, toasted
  small bunch fresh coriander
    (cilantro), chopped
  fresh Thai sweet basil leaves,
    to garnish
For the dressing
  300ml/½ pint/1¼ cups water
  10ml/2 tsp shrimp paste
  15ml/1 tbsp palm sugar or light
    muscovado (brown) sugar
  2 kaffir lime leaves, torn into
    small pieces
  ½ lemon grass stalk, sliced

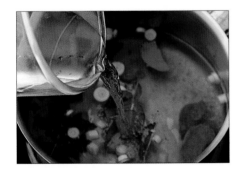

**1** Make the dressing. Put the measured water in a small pan with the shrimp paste, sugar, kaffir lime leaves and lemon grass. Heat gently, stirring, until the sugar dissolves, then bring to boiling point and simmer for 5 minutes. Strain into a bowl and set aside until cold.

**2** Put the cooked rice in a large salad bowl and fluff up the grains with a fork. Add the Asian pear, dried shrimp, avocado, cucumber, lemon grass and sweet chilli sauce. Mix well.

**3** Add the diced chilli, almonds and coriander to the bowl and toss well. Garnish with Thai basil leaves and serve with the bowl of dressing to spoon over the top of individual portions.

# SCENTED FISH SALAD

*FOR A TROPICAL TASTE OF THE FAR EAST, TRY THIS DELICIOUS FISH SALAD SCENTED WITH COCONUT, FRUIT AND WARM THAI SPICES. DO TRY TO LOCATE THE PITAYA OR DRAGON FRUIT. THE FLESH OF THESE FUCHSIA-PINK OR YELLOW EXOTICS IS SWEET AND REFRESHING, WITH A SLIGHTLY ACIDIC MELON-LIKE FLAVOUR THAT GOES PARTICULARLY WELL WITH FISH.*

SERVES FOUR

INGREDIENTS
    350g/12oz fillet of red mullet, sea
        bream or snapper
    1 cos or romaine lettuce
    1 papaya or mango, peeled
        and sliced
    1 pitaya, peeled and sliced
    1 large ripe tomato, cut into wedges
    ½ cucumber, peeled and cut
        into batons
    3 spring onions (scallions), sliced
    salt
For the marinade
    5ml/1 tsp coriander seeds
    5ml/1 tsp fennel seeds
    2.5ml/½ tsp cumin seeds
    5ml/1 tsp caster (superfine) sugar
    2.5ml/½ tsp hot chilli sauce
    30ml/2 tbsp garlic oil
For the dressing
    15ml/1 tbsp creamed coconut
        (coconut cream)
    45ml/3 tbsp boiling water
    60ml/4 tbsp groundnut (peanut) oil
    finely grated rind and juice of 1 lime
    1 fresh red chilli, seeded and
        finely chopped
    5ml/1 tsp granulated sugar
    45ml/3 tbsp chopped fresh
        coriander (cilantro)

**1** Cut the fish into even strips, removing any stray bones. Place it on a plate.

**2** Make the marinade. Put the coriander, fennel and cumin seeds in a mortar. Add the sugar and crush with a pestle. Stir in the chilli sauce, garlic oil, and salt to taste and mix to a paste.

**3** Spread the paste over the fish, cover and leave to marinate in a cool place for at least 20 minutes.

**4** Make the dressing. Place the coconut and salt in a screw-top jar. Stir in the water. Add the oil, lime rind and juice, chilli, sugar and coriander. Shake well.

**5** Wash and dry the lettuce leaves. Place in a bowl and add the papaya or mango, pitaya, tomato, cucumber and spring onions. Pour in the dressing and toss well to coat.

**6** Heat a large non-stick frying-pan, add the fish and cook for 5 minutes, turning once. Add the cooked fish to the salad, toss lightly and serve immediately.

**COOK'S TIPS**
• If planning ahead, you can leave the fish in its marinade for up to 8 hours in the refrigerator. The dressing can also be made in advance, but do not add the fresh coriander (cilantro) until the last minute and shake vigorously again before pouring it over the salad.
• To make garlic oil, heat 120ml/4fl oz/ ½ cup bland-flavoured oil, such as sunflower, in a small pan. Add 30ml/ 2 tbsp crushed garlic and cook gently for 5 minutes, until the garlic is pale gold. Do not let it burn or the oil will taste bitter. Cool, strain into a clean screw-top jar and use as required.

# PAK CHOI <u>WITH</u> LIME DRESSING

*THE COCONUT DRESSING FOR THIS THAI SPECIALITY IS TRADITIONALLY MADE USING FISH SAUCE, BUT VEGETARIANS COULD USE MUSHROOM SAUCE INSTEAD. BEWARE, THIS IS A FIERY DISH!*

### SERVES FOUR

INGREDIENTS
  30ml/2 tbsp oil
  3 fresh red chillies, cut into
    thin strips
  4 garlic cloves, thinly sliced
  6 spring onions (scallions),
    sliced diagonally
  2 pak choi (bok choy), shredded
  15ml/1 tbsp crushed peanuts
For the dressing
  30ml/2 tbsp fresh lime juice
  15–30ml/1–2 tbsp Thai fish sauce
  250ml/8fl oz/1 cup coconut milk

**1** Make the dressing. Put the lime juice and fish sauce in a bowl and mix well together, then gradually whisk in the coconut milk until combined.

**2** Heat the oil in a wok and stir-fry the chillies for 2–3 minutes, until crisp. Transfer to a plate using a slotted spoon. Add the garlic to the wok and stir-fry for 30–60 seconds, until golden brown. Transfer to the plate.

**3** Stir-fry the white parts of the spring onions for about 2–3 minutes, then add the green parts and stir-fry for 1 minute more. Transfer to the plate.

**4** Bring a large pan of lightly salted water to the boil and add the pak choi. Stir twice, then drain immediately.

**5** Place the pak choi in a large bowl, add the dressing and toss to mix. Spoon into a large serving bowl and sprinkle with the crushed peanuts and the stir-fried chilli mixture. Serve warm or cold.

**VARIATION**
If you don't like particularly spicy food, substitute red (bell) pepper strips for some or all of the chillies.

# SOUTHERN-STYLE YAM

*THE FOOD OF THE SOUTHERN REGION IS NOTORIOUSLY HOT AND BECAUSE OF THE PROXIMITY TO THE BORDERS WITH MALAYSIA, THAILAND'S MUSLIM MINORITY ARE MOSTLY TO BE FOUND IN THIS AREA. THEY HAVE INTRODUCED RICHER CURRY FLAVOURS REMINISCENT OF INDIAN FOOD.*

SERVES FOUR

INGREDIENTS
   90g/3½oz Chinese leaves (Chinese
     cabbage), shredded
   90g/3½oz/generous 1 cup
     beansprouts
   90g/3½oz/scant 1 cup green
     beans, trimmed
   90g/3½oz broccoli, preferably the
     purple sprouting variety, divided
     into florets
   15ml/1 tbsp sesame seeds, toasted
For the yam
   60ml/4 tbsp coconut cream
   5ml/1 tsp Thai red curry paste
   90g/3½oz/1¼ cups oyster
     mushrooms or field
     (portabello) mushrooms, sliced
   60ml/4 tbsp coconut milk
   5ml/1 tsp ground turmeric
   5ml/1 tsp thick tamarind juice, made
     by mixing tamarind paste with
     warm water
   juice of ½ lemon
   60ml/4 tbsp light soy sauce
   5ml/1 tsp palm sugar or light
     muscovado (brown) sugar

**1** Steam the shredded Chinese leaves, beansprouts, green beans and broccoli separately or blanch them in boiling water for 1 minute per batch. Drain, place in a serving bowl and leave to cool.

**2** Make the yam. Pour the coconut cream into a wok or frying pan and heat gently for 2–3 minutes, until it separates. Stir in the red curry paste. Cook over a low heat for 30 seconds, until the mixture is fragrant.

**3** Increase the heat to high and add the mushrooms to the wok or pan. Cook for a further 2–3 minutes.

**4** Pour in the coconut milk and add the ground turmeric, tamarind juice, lemon juice, soy sauce and sugar to the wok or pan. Mix thoroughly.

**5** Pour the mixture over the prepared vegetables and toss well to combine. Sprinkle with the toasted sesame seeds and serve immediately.

**COOK'S TIPS**
• There's no need to buy coconut cream especially for this dish. Use a carton or can of coconut milk. Skim the cream off the top and cook 60ml/4 tbsp of it before adding the curry paste. Add the measured coconut milk later, as described in the recipe.
• Oyster mushrooms may have fawn, peacock-blue or yellow caps, depending on the variety.

# STEAMED MORNING GLORY WITH FRIED GARLIC AND SHALLOTS

*MORNING GLORY GOES BY VARIOUS NAMES, INCLUDING WATER SPINACH, WATER CONVOLVULUS AND SWAMP CABBAGE. IT IS A GREEN LEAFY VEGETABLE WITH LONG JOINTED STEMS AND ARROW-SHAPED LEAVES. THE STEMS REMAIN CRUNCHY WHILE THE LEAVES WILT LIKE SPINACH WHEN COOKED.*

**SERVES FOUR**

### INGREDIENTS
2 bunches morning glory, total weight about 250g/9oz, trimmed and coarsely chopped into 2.5cm/1in lengths
30ml/2 tbsp vegetable oil
4 shallots, thinly sliced
6 large garlic cloves, thinly sliced
sea salt
1.5ml/¼ tsp dried chilli flakes

**VARIATIONS**
Use spinach instead of morning glory, or substitute young spring greens (collards), sprouting broccoli or Swiss chard.

**1** Place the morning glory in a steamer and steam over a pan of boiling water for 30 seconds, until just wilted. If necessary, cook it in batches. Place the leaves in a bowl or spread them out on a large serving plate.

**2** Heat the oil in a wok and stir-fry the shallots and garlic over a medium to high heat until golden. Spoon the mixture over the morning glory, sprinkle with a little sea salt and the chilli flakes and serve immediately.

# STIR-FRIED PINEAPPLE WITH GINGER

*THIS DISH MAKES AN INTERESTING ACCOMPANIMENT TO GRILLED MEAT OR STRONGLY-FLAVOURED FISH SUCH AS TUNA OR SWORDFISH. IF THE IDEA SEEMS STRANGE, THINK OF IT AS RESEMBLING A FRESH MANGO CHUTNEY, BUT WITH PINEAPPLE AS THE PRINCIPAL INGREDIENT.*

SERVES FOUR

INGREDIENTS

1 pineapple
15ml/1 tbsp vegetable oil
2 garlic cloves, finely chopped
2 shallots, finely chopped
5cm/2in piece fresh root ginger,
  peeled and finely shredded
30ml/2 tbsp light soy sauce
juice of ½ lime
1 large fresh red chilli, seeded and
  finely shredded

**VARIATION**
This also tastes excellent if peaches or nectarines are substituted for the diced pineapple. Use three or four, depending on their size.

1 Trim and peel the pineapple. Cut out the core and dice the flesh.

2 Heat the oil in a wok or frying pan. Stir-fry the garlic and shallots over a medium heat for 2–3 minutes, until golden. Do not let the garlic burn or the dish will taste bitter.

3 Add the pineapple. Stir-fry for about 2 minutes, or until the pineapple cubes start to turn golden on the edges.

4 Add the ginger, soy sauce, lime juice and chopped chilli. Toss together until well mixed. Cook over a low heat for a further 2 minutes, then serve.

# CURRIES

*Thai curries are based on wet pastes, rather than dry spice mixtures, with chillies, garlic, shallots, ginger and galangal the predominant flavourings. Fresh lemon grass and kaffir lime leaves are often included, and coconut is what marries the various ingredients together. The majority of meat and poultry dishes in Thailand are curries, and vegetable versions are also very popular. The typically Thai citrus flavours work particularly well in fish and shellfish curries.*

# VEGETABLE FOREST CURRY

*THIS IS A THIN, SOUPY CURRY WITH LOTS OF FRESH GREEN VEGETABLES AND ROBUST FLAVOURS. IN THE FORESTED REGIONS OF THAILAND, WHERE IT ORIGINATED, IT WOULD BE MADE USING EDIBLE WILD LEAVES AND ROOTS. SERVE IT WITH RICE OR NOODLES FOR A SIMPLE LUNCH OR SUPPER.*

### SERVES TWO

INGREDIENTS
  600ml/1 pint/2½ cups water
  5ml/1 tsp Thai red curry paste
  5cm/2in piece fresh galangal or fresh
    root ginger
  90g/3½ oz/scant 1 cup green beans
  2 kaffir lime leaves, torn
  8 baby corn cobs,
    halved widthways
  2 heads Chinese broccoli, chopped
  90g/3½ oz/generous 3 cups
    beansprouts
  15ml/1 tbsp drained bottled green
    peppercorns, crushed
  10ml/2 tsp granulated sugar
  5ml/1 tsp salt

**1** Heat the water in a large pan. Add the red curry paste and stir until it has dissolved completely. Bring to the boil.

**2** Meanwhile, using a sharp knife, peel and finely chop the fresh galangal or root ginger.

**3** Add the galangal or ginger, green beans, lime leaves, baby corn cobs, broccoli and beansprouts to the pan. Stir in the crushed peppercorns, sugar and salt. Bring back to the boil, then reduce the heat to low and simmer for 2 minutes. Serve immediately.

# TOFU <u>AND</u> GREEN BEAN RED CURRY

*THIS IS ONE OF THOSE VERSATILE RECIPES THAT SHOULD BE IN EVERY COOK'S REPERTOIRE. THIS VERSION USES GREEN BEANS, BUT OTHER TYPES OF VEGETABLE WORK EQUALLY WELL. THE TOFU TAKES ON THE FLAVOUR OF THE SPICE PASTE AND ALSO BOOSTS THE NUTRITIONAL VALUE.*

SERVES FOUR TO SIX

INGREDIENTS
  600ml/1 pint/2½ cups canned
    coconut milk
  15ml/1 tbsp Thai red curry paste
  45ml/3 tbsp Thai fish sauce
  10ml/2 tsp palm sugar or light
    muscovado (brown) sugar
  225g/8oz/3¼ cups button
    (white) mushrooms
  115g/4oz/scant 1 cup green
    beans, trimmed
  175g/6oz firm tofu, rinsed, drained
    and cut in 2cm/¾ in cubes
  4 kaffir lime leaves, torn
  2 fresh red chillies, seeded
    and sliced
  fresh coriander (cilantro) leaves,
    to garnish

**1** Pour about one-third of the coconut milk into a wok or pan. Cook until it starts to separate and an oily sheen appears on the surface.

**2** Add the red curry paste, fish sauce and sugar to the coconut milk. Mix thoroughly, then add the mushrooms. Stir and cook for 1 minute.

**3** Stir in the remaining coconut milk. Bring back to the boil, then add the green beans and tofu cubes. Simmer gently for 4–5 minutes more.

**4** Stir in the kaffir lime leaves and sliced red chillies. Spoon the curry into a serving dish, garnish with the coriander leaves and serve immediately.

# CURRIED SEAFOOD WITH COCONUT MILK

*THIS CURRY IS BASED ON A THAI CLASSIC. THE LOVELY GREEN COLOUR IS IMPARTED BY THE FINELY CHOPPED CHILLI AND FRESH HERBS ADDED DURING THE LAST FEW MOMENTS OF COOKING.*

### SERVES FOUR

INGREDIENTS

   225g/8oz small ready-prepared squid
   225g/8oz raw tiger prawns
     (jumbo shrimp)
   400ml/14fl oz/1⅔ cups coconut milk
   2 kaffir lime leaves, finely shredded
   30ml/2 tbsp Thai fish sauce
   450g/1lb firm white fish fillets,
     skinned, boned and cut into chunks
   2 fresh green chillies, seeded and
     finely chopped
   30ml/2 tbsp torn fresh basil or
     coriander (cilantro) leaves
   squeeze of fresh lime juice
   cooked Thai jasmine rice,
     to serve
For the curry paste
   6 spring onions (scallions),
     coarsely chopped
   4 fresh coriander (cilantro) stems,
     coarsely chopped, plus 45ml/3 tbsp
     chopped fresh coriander (cilantro)
   4 kaffir lime leaves, shredded
   8 fresh green chillies, seeded and
     coarsely chopped
   1 lemon grass stalk,
     coarsely chopped
   2.5cm/1in piece fresh root ginger,
     peeled and coarsely chopped
   45ml/3 tbsp chopped fresh basil
   15ml/1 tbsp vegetable oil

**1** Make the curry paste. Put all the ingredients, except the oil, in a food processor and process to a paste. Alternatively, pound together in a mortar with a pestle. Stir in the oil.

**2** Rinse the squid and pat dry with kitchen paper. Cut the bodies into rings and halve the tentacles, if necessary.

**3** Heat a wok until hot, add the prawns and stir-fry, without any oil, for about 4 minutes, until they turn pink.

**4** Remove the prawns from the wok and leave to cool slightly, then peel off the shells, saving a few with shells on for the garnish. Make a slit along the back of each one and remove the black vein.

**5** Pour the coconut milk into the wok, then bring to the boil over a medium heat, stirring constantly. Add 30ml/ 2 tbsp of curry paste, the shredded lime leaves and fish sauce and stir well to mix. Reduce the heat to low and simmer gently for about 10 minutes.

**6** Add the squid, prawns and chunks of fish and cook for about 2 minutes, until the seafood is tender. Take care not to overcook the squid as it will become tough very quickly.

**7** Just before serving, stir in the chillies and basil or coriander. Taste and adjust the flavour with a squeeze of lime juice. Garnish with prawns in their shells, and serve with Thai jasmine rice.

### VARIATIONS

• You can use any firm-fleshed white fish for this curry, such as monkfish, cod, haddock or John Dory.
• If you prefer, you could substitute shelled scallops for the squid. Slice them in half horizontally and add them with the prawns (shrimp). As with the squid, be careful not to overcook them.

# CHICKEN AND LEMON GRASS CURRY

*THIS FRAGRANT AND TRULY DELICIOUS CURRY IS EXCEPTIONALLY EASY AND TAKES LESS THAN TWENTY MINUTES TO PREPARE AND COOK — A PERFECT MID-WEEK MEAL.*

**SERVES FOUR**

INGREDIENTS
  45ml/3 tbsp vegetable oil
  2 garlic cloves, crushed
  500g/1¼ lb skinless, boneless
    chicken thighs, chopped into
    small pieces
  45ml/3 tbsp Thai fish sauce
  120ml/4fl oz/½ cup
    chicken stock
  5ml/1 tsp granulated sugar
  1 lemon grass stalk, chopped into
    4 sticks and lightly crushed
  5 kaffir lime leaves, rolled into
    cylinders and thinly sliced across,
    plus extra to garnish
chopped roasted peanuts
  and chopped fresh coriander
  (cilantro), to garnish
For the curry paste
  1 lemon grass stalk,
    coarsely chopped
  2.5cm/1in piece fresh galangal,
    peeled and coarsely chopped
  2 kaffir lime leaves, chopped
  3 shallots, coarsely chopped
  6 coriander (cilantro) roots,
    coarsely chopped
  2 garlic cloves
  2 fresh green chillies, seeded and
    coarsely chopped
  5ml/1 tsp shrimp paste
  5ml/1 tsp ground turmeric

**1** Make the curry paste. Place all the ingredients in a large mortar, or food processor and pound with a pestle or process to a smooth paste.

**2** Heat the vegetable oil in a wok or large, heavy frying pan, add the garlic and cook over a low heat, stirring frequently, until golden brown. Be careful not to let the garlic burn or it will taste bitter. Add the curry paste and stir-fry with the garlic for about 30 seconds more.

**3** Add the chicken pieces to the pan and stir until thoroughly coated with the curry paste. Stir in the Thai fish sauce and chicken stock, with the sugar, and cook, stirring constantly, for 2 minutes more.

**4** Add the lemon grass and lime leaves, reduce the heat and simmer for 10 minutes. If the mixture begins to dry out, add a little more stock or water.

**5** Remove the lemon grass, if you like. Spoon the curry into four dishes, garnish with the lime leaves, peanuts and coriander and serve immediately.

# YELLOW CHICKEN CURRY

*THE PAIRING OF SLIGHTLY SWEET COCONUT MILK AND FRUIT WITH SAVOURY CHICKEN AND SPICES IS AT ONCE A COMFORTING, REFRESHING AND EXOTIC COMBINATION.*

SERVES FOUR

INGREDIENTS

    300ml/½ pint/1¼ cups
      chicken stock
    30ml/2 tbsp thick tamarind juice,
      made by mixing tamarind paste with
      warm water
    15ml/1 tbsp granulated sugar
    200ml/7fl oz/scant 1 cup
      coconut milk
    1 green papaya, peeled, seeded and
      thinly sliced
    250g/9oz skinless, boneless chicken
      breast portions, diced
    juice of 1 lime
    lime slices, to garnish
For the curry paste
    1 fresh red chilli, seeded and
      coarsely chopped
    4 garlic cloves, coarsely chopped
    3 shallots, coarsely chopped
    2 lemon grass stalks, sliced
    5cm/2in piece fresh turmeric,
      coarsely chopped, or 5ml/1 tsp
      ground turmeric
    5ml/1 tsp shrimp paste
    5ml/1 tsp salt

**1** Make the yellow curry paste. Put the red chilli, garlic, shallots, lemon grass and turmeric in a mortar or food processor. Add the shrimp paste and salt. Pound or process to a paste, adding a little water if necessary.

**COOK'S TIP**
Fresh turmeric resembles root ginger in appearance and is a member of the same family. When preparing it, wear gloves to protect your hands from staining.

**2** Pour the stock into a wok or medium pan and bring it to the boil. Stir in the curry paste. Bring back to the boil and add the tamarind juice, sugar and coconut milk. Add the papaya and chicken and cook over a medium to high heat for about 15 minutes, stirring frequently, until the chicken is cooked.

**3** Stir in the lime juice, transfer to a warm dish and serve immediately, garnished with lime slices.

# SOUTHERN CHICKEN CURRY

*A MILD COCONUT CURRY FLAVOURED WITH TURMERIC, CORIANDER AND CUMIN SEEDS THAT DEMONSTRATES THE INFLUENCE OF MALAYSIAN COOKING ON THAI CUISINE.*

SERVES FOUR

INGREDIENTS

  60ml/4 tbsp vegetable oil
  1 large garlic clove, crushed
  1 chicken, weighing about 1.5kg/
    3–3½lb, chopped into
    12 large pieces
  400ml/14fl oz/1⅔ cups
    coconut cream
  250ml/8fl oz/1 cup chicken stock
  30ml/2 tbsp Thai fish sauce
  30ml/2 tbsp sugar
  juice of 2 limes
To garnish
  2 small fresh red chillies, seeded and
    finely chopped
  1 bunch spring onions (scallions),
    thinly sliced
For the curry paste
  5ml/1 tsp dried chilli flakes
  2.5ml/½ tsp salt
  5cm/2in piece fresh turmeric or
    5ml/1 tsp ground turmeric
  2.5ml/½ tsp coriander seeds
  2.5ml/½ tsp cumin seeds
  5ml/1 tsp dried shrimp paste

**1** First make the curry paste. Put all the ingredients in a mortar, food processor or spice grinder and pound, process or grind to a smooth paste.

**2** Heat the oil in a wok or frying pan and cook the garlic until golden. Add the chicken and cook until golden. Remove the chicken and set aside.

**3** Reheat the oil and add the curry paste and then half the coconut cream. Cook for a few minutes until fragrant.

**4** Return the chicken to the wok or pan, add the stock, mixing well, then add the remaining coconut cream, the fish sauce, sugar and lime juice. Stir well and bring to the boil, then lower the heat and simmer for 15 minutes.

**5** Turn the curry into four warm serving bowls and sprinkle with the chopped fresh chillies and spring onions to garnish. Serve immediately.

**COOK'S TIP**
Use a large sharp knife or a Chinese cleaver to chop the chicken into pieces. Wash the board, knife and your hands thoroughly afterwards in hot, soapy water as chicken is notorious for harbouring harmful micro-organisms and bacteria.

# JUNGLE CURRY OF GUINEA FOWL

*A TRADITIONAL WILD FOOD COUNTRY CURRY FROM THE NORTH-CENTRAL REGION OF THAILAND, THIS DISH CAN BE MADE USING ANY GAME, FISH OR CHICKEN. GUINEA FOWL IS NOT TYPICAL OF THAI CUISINE, BUT IS A POPULAR AND WIDELY AVAILABLE GAME BIRD IN THE WEST.*

SERVES FOUR

INGREDIENTS

   1 guinea fowl or similar game bird
   15ml/1 tbsp vegetable oil
   10ml/2 tsp green curry paste
   15ml/1 tbsp Thai fish sauce
   2.5cm/1in piece fresh galangal,
     peeled and finely chopped
   15ml/1 tbsp fresh green peppercorns
   3 kaffir lime leaves, torn
   15ml/1 tbsp whisky,
     preferably Mekhong
   300ml/½ pint/1¼ cups
     chicken stock
   50g/2oz snake beans or yard-long
     beans, cut into 2.5cm/1in lengths
     (about ½ cup)
   225g/8oz/3¼ cups chestnut
     mushrooms, sliced
   1 piece drained canned bamboo
     shoot, about 50g/2oz, shredded
   5ml/1 tsp dried chilli flakes, to
     garnish (optional)

**1** Cut up the guinea fowl, remove and discard the skin, then take all the meat off the bones. Chop the meat into bitesize pieces and set aside.

**2** Heat the oil in a wok or frying pan and add the curry paste. Stir-fry over a medium heat for 30 seconds, until the paste gives off its aroma.

**3** Add the fish sauce and the guinea fowl meat and stir-fry until the meat is browned all over. Add the galangal, peppercorns, lime leaves and whisky, then pour in the stock.

**4** Bring to the boil. Add the vegetables, return to a simmer and cook gently for 2–3 minutes, until they are just cooked. Spoon into a dish, sprinkle with chilli flakes, if you like, and serve.

**COOK'S TIPS**
• Guinea fowl originated in West Africa and was regarded as a game bird. However, it has been domesticated in Europe for over 500 years. They range in size from 675g/1½lb to 2kg/4½lb, but about 1.2kg/2½lb is average. American readers could substitute two or three Cornish hens, depending on size.
• Fresh green peppercorns are simply unripe berries. They are sold on the stem and look rather like miniature Brussels sprout stalks. Look for them at Thai supermarkets. If unavailable, substitute bottled green peppercorns, but rinse well and drain them first.

# PORK AND PINEAPPLE COCONUT CURRY

*THE HEAT OF THIS CURRY BALANCES OUT ITS SWEETNESS TO MAKE A SMOOTH AND FRAGRANT DISH. IT TAKES VERY LITTLE TIME TO COOK, SO IS IDEAL FOR A QUICK SUPPER BEFORE GOING OUT OR FOR A MID-WEEK FAMILY MEAL ON A BUSY EVENING.*

SERVES FOUR

INGREDIENTS

    400ml/14fl oz can or carton
      coconut milk
    10ml/2 tsp Thai red
      curry paste
    400g/14oz pork loin steaks,
      trimmed and thinly sliced
    15ml/1 tbsp Thai fish sauce
    5ml/1 tsp palm sugar or light
      muscovado (brown) sugar
    15ml/1 tbsp tamarind juice, made
      by mixing tamarind paste with
      warm water
    2 kaffir lime leaves, torn
    ½ medium pineapple, peeled
      and chopped
    1 fresh red chilli, seeded and
      finely chopped

**1** Pour the coconut milk into a bowl and let it settle, so that the cream rises to the surface. Scoop the cream into a measuring jug (cup). You should have about 250ml/8fl oz/1 cup. If necessary, add a little of the coconut milk.

**2** Pour the coconut cream into a large pan and bring it to the boil.

**3** Cook the coconut cream for about 10 minutes, until the cream separates, stirring frequently to prevent it from sticking to the base of the pan and scorching. Add the red curry paste and stir until well mixed. Cook, stirring occasionally, for about 4 minutes, until the paste is fragrant.

**4** Add the sliced pork and stir in the fish sauce, sugar and tamarind juice. Cook, stirring constantly, for 1–2 minutes, until the sugar has dissolved and the pork is no longer pink.

**5** Add the remaining coconut milk and the lime leaves. Bring to the boil, then stir in the pineapple. Reduce the heat and simmer gently for 3 minutes, or until the pork is fully cooked. Sprinkle over the chilli and serve.

# CURRIED PORK WITH PICKLED GARLIC

*THIS VERY RICH CURRY IS BEST ACCOMPANIED BY LOTS OF PLAIN RICE AND PERHAPS A LIGHT VEGETABLE DISH. IT COULD SERVE FOUR IF SERVED WITH A VEGETABLE CURRY. ASIAN STORES SELL PICKLED GARLIC. IT IS WELL WORTH INVESTING IN A JAR, AS THE TASTE IS SWEET AND DELICIOUS.*

SERVES TWO

INGREDIENTS

130g/4½oz lean pork steaks
30ml/2 tbsp vegetable oil
1 garlic clove, crushed
15ml/1 tbsp Thai red curry paste
130ml/4½fl oz/generous ½ cup
  coconut cream
2.5cm/1in piece fresh root ginger,
  finely chopped
30ml/2 tbsp vegetable or
  chicken stock
30ml/2 tbsp Thai fish sauce
5ml/1 tsp granulated sugar
2.5ml/½ tsp ground turmeric
10ml/2 tsp lemon juice
4 pickled garlic cloves,
  finely chopped
strips of lemon and lime rind,
  to garnish

**1** Place the pork steaks in the freezer for 30–40 minutes, until firm, then, using a sharp knife, cut the meat into fine slivers, trimming off any excess fat.

**2** Heat the oil in a wok or large, heavy frying pan and cook the garlic over a low to medium heat until golden brown. Do not let it burn. Add the curry paste and stir it in well.

**3** Add the coconut cream and stir until the liquid begins to reduce and thicken. Stir in the pork. Cook for 2 minutes more, until the pork is cooked through.

**4** Add the ginger, stock, fish sauce, sugar and turmeric, stirring constantly, then add the lemon juice and pickled garlic. Spoon into bowls, garnish with strips of rind, and serve.

# GREEN BEEF CURRY WITH THAI AUBERGINES

*THIS IS A VERY QUICK CURRY SO BE SURE TO USE GOOD QUALITY MEAT. SIRLOIN IS RECOMMENDED, BUT TENDER RUMP (ROUND) STEAK COULD BE USED INSTEAD.*

### SERVES FOUR TO SIX

INGREDIENTS
  450g/1lb beef sirloin
  15ml/1 tbsp vegetable oil
  45ml/3 tbsp Thai green curry paste
  600ml/1 pint/2½ cups coconut milk
  4 kaffir lime leaves, torn
  15–30ml/1–2 tbsp Thai fish sauce
  5ml/1 tsp palm sugar or light
    muscovado (brown) sugar
  150g/5oz small Thai aubergines
    (eggplant), halved
  a small handful of fresh Thai basil
  2 fresh green chillies, to garnish

**1** Trim off any excess fat from the beef. Using a sharp knife, cut it into long, thin strips. This is easiest to do if it is well chilled. Set it aside.

**2** Heat the oil in a large, heavy pan or wok. Add the curry paste and cook for 1–2 minutes, until it is fragrant.

**3** Stir in half the coconut milk, a little at a time. Cook, stirring frequently, for about 5–6 minutes, until an oily sheen appears on the surface of the liquid.

**4** Add the beef to the pan with the kaffir lime leaves, Thai fish sauce, sugar and aubergine halves. Cook for 2–3 minutes, then stir in the remaining coconut milk.

**5** Bring back to a simmer and cook until the meat and aubergines are tender. Stir in the Thai basil just before serving. Finely shred the green chillies and use to garnish the curry.

**COOK'S TIP**
To make the green curry paste, put 15 fresh green chillies, 2 chopped lemon grass stalks, 3 sliced shallots, 2 garlic cloves, 15ml/1 tbsp chopped galangal, 4 chopped kaffir lime leaves, 2.5ml/ ½ tsp grated kaffir lime rind, 5ml/1 tsp chopped coriander root, 6 black peppercorns, 5ml/1 tsp each roasted coriander and cumin seeds, 15ml/1 tbsp granulated sugar, 5ml/1 tsp salt and 5ml/1 tsp shrimp paste into a food processor and process until smooth. Gradually add 30ml/2 tbsp vegetable oil, processing after each addition.

# THICK BEEF CURRY IN SWEET PEANUT SAUCE

*THIS CURRY IS DELICIOUSLY RICH AND THICKER THAN MOST OTHER THAI CURRIES. SERVE IT WITH BOILED JASMINE RICE AND SALTED DUCK'S EGGS, IF YOU LIKE.*

### SERVES FOUR TO SIX

INGREDIENTS
   600ml/1 pint/2½ cups coconut milk
   45ml/3 tbsp Thai red curry paste
   45ml/3 tbsp Thai fish sauce
   30ml/2 tbsp palm sugar or light
      muscovado (brown) sugar
   2 lemon grass stalks, bruised
   450g/1lb rump (round) steak, cut
      into thin strips
   75g/3oz/¾ cup roasted
      peanuts, ground
   2 fresh red chillies, sliced
   5 kaffir lime leaves, torn
   salt and ground black pepper
   2 salted eggs, cut in wedges, and
      10–15 Thai basil leaves, to garnish

**1** Pour half the coconut milk into a large, heavy pan. Place over a medium heat and bring to the boil, stirring constantly until the milk separates.

**2** Stir in the red curry paste and cook for 2–3 minutes until the mixture is fragrant and thoroughly blended. Add the fish sauce, sugar and bruised lemon grass stalks. Mix well.

**3** Continue to cook until the colour deepens. Gradually add the remaining coconut milk, stirring constantly. Bring back to the boil.

**COOK'S TIP**
If you don't have the time to make your own red curry paste, you can buy a ready-made Thai curry paste. There is a wide range available in most Asian stores and large supermarkets.

**4** Add the beef and peanuts. Cook, stirring constantly, for 8–10 minutes, or until most of the liquid has evaporated. Add the chillies and lime leaves. Season to taste and serve, garnished with wedges of salted eggs and Thai basil leaves.

# STIR-FRIES

After a busy day at work, a quick-and-easy stir-fry is just the thing for a tasty and healthy supper. Bitesize pieces of food are tossed over a high heat in a wok or large frying pan, searing the outside. Only a small quantity of oil is used and the ingredients retain all of their colour, flavour and goodness. Here you will find recipes for pork, beef, poultry and vegetable stir-fries, flavoured with typical Thai ingredients such as ginger, galangal, chillies and lemon grass.

# STIR-FRIED CRISPY TOFU

*THE ASPARAGUS GROWN IN ASIA TENDS TO HAVE SLENDER STALKS. LOOK FOR IT IN THAI MARKETS OR SUBSTITUTE THE THIN ASPARAGUS POPULARLY KNOWN AS SPRUE.*

SERVES TWO

INGREDIENTS

   250g/9oz fried tofu cubes
   30ml/2 tbsp groundnut (peanut) oil
   15ml/1 tbsp Thai green curry paste
   30ml/2 tbsp light soy sauce
   2 kaffir lime leaves, rolled into
     cylinders and thinly sliced
   30ml/2 tbsp granulated sugar
   150ml/¼ pint/⅔ cup vegetable stock
   250g/9oz Asian asparagus, trimmed
     and sliced into 5cm/2in lengths
   30ml/2 tbsp roasted peanuts,
     finely chopped

**VARIATION**
Substitute slim carrot sticks or broccoli florets for the asparagus.

**1** Preheat the grill (broiler) to medium. Place the tofu cubes in a grill pan and grill (broil) for 2–3 minutes, then turn them over and continue to cook until they are crisp and golden brown all over. Watch them carefully; they must not be allowed to burn.

**2** Heat the oil in a wok or heavy frying pan. Add the green curry paste and cook over a medium heat, stirring constantly, for 1–2 minutes, until it gives off its aroma.

**3** Stir the soy sauce, lime leaves, sugar and vegetable stock into the wok or pan and mix well. Bring to the boil, then reduce the heat to low so that the mixture is just simmering.

**4** Add the asparagus and simmer gently for 5 minutes. Meanwhile, chop each piece of tofu into four, then add to the pan with the peanuts.

**5** Toss to coat all the ingredients in the sauce, then spoon into a warmed dish and serve immediately.

# STIR-FRIED SEEDS AND VEGETABLES

*THE CONTRAST BETWEEN THE CRUNCHY SEEDS AND VEGETABLES AND THE RICH, SAVOURY SAUCE IS WHAT MAKES THIS DISH SO DELICIOUS. SERVE IT SOLO, OR WITH RICE OR NOODLES.*

**SERVES FOUR**

**INGREDIENTS**
30ml/2 tbsp vegetable oil
30ml/2 tbsp sesame seeds
30ml/2 tbsp sunflower seeds
30ml/2 tbsp pumpkin seeds
2 garlic cloves, finely chopped
2.5cm/1in piece fresh root ginger, peeled and finely chopped
2 large carrots, cut into batons
2 large courgettes (zucchini), cut into batons
90g/3½oz/1½ cups oyster mushrooms, torn in pieces
150g/5oz watercress or spinach leaves, coarsely chopped
small bunch fresh mint or coriander (cilantro), leaves and stems chopped
60ml/4 tbsp black bean sauce
30ml/2 tbsp light soy sauce
15ml/1 tbsp palm sugar or light muscovado (brown) sugar
30ml/2 tbsp rice vinegar

**1** Heat the oil in a wok or large frying pan. Add the seeds. Toss over a medium heat for 1 minute, then add the garlic and ginger and continue to stir-fry until the ginger is aromatic and the garlic is golden. Do not let the garlic burn or it will taste bitter.

**2** Add the carrot and courgette batons and the sliced mushrooms to the wok or pan and stir-fry over a medium heat for a further 5 minutes, or until all the vegetables are crisp-tender and are golden at the edges.

**3** Add the watercress or spinach with the fresh herbs. Toss over the heat for 1 minute, then stir in the black bean sauce, soy sauce, sugar and vinegar. Stir-fry for 1–2 minutes, until combined and hot. Serve immediately.

**COOK'S TIP**
Oyster mushrooms have acquired their name because of their texture, rather than flavour, which is quite superb. They are delicate, so it is usually better to tear them into pieces along the lines of the gills, rather than slice them with a knife.

# FRAGRANT MUSHROOMS IN LETTUCE LEAVES

*THIS QUICK AND EASY VEGETABLE DISH IS SERVED ON LETTUCE LEAF "SAUCERS" SO CAN BE EATEN WITH THE FINGERS — A GREAT TREAT FOR CHILDREN.*

### SERVES TWO

INGREDIENTS
30ml/2 tbsp vegetable oil
2 garlic cloves, finely chopped
2 baby cos or romaine lettuces,
   or 2 Little Gem (Bibb) lettuces
1 lemon grass stalk, finely chopped
2 kaffir lime leaves, rolled in
   cylinders and thinly sliced
200g/7oz/3 cups oyster or chestnut
   mushrooms, sliced
1 small fresh red chilli, seeded
   and finely chopped
juice of ½ lemon
30ml/2 tbsp light soy sauce
5ml/1 tsp palm sugar or light
   muscovado (brown) sugar
small bunch fresh mint, leaves
   removed from the stalks

**1** Heat the oil in a wok or frying pan. Add the garlic and cook over a medium heat, stirring occasionally, until golden. Do not let it burn or it will taste bitter.

**2** Meanwhile, separate the individual lettuce leaves and set aside.

**3** Increase the heat under the wok or pan and add the lemon grass, lime leaves and sliced mushrooms. Stir-fry for about 2 minutes.

**4** Add the chilli, lemon juice, soy sauce and sugar to the wok or pan. Toss the mixture over the heat to combine the ingredients together, then stir-fry for a further 2 minutes.

**5** Arrange the lettuce leaves on a large plate. Spoon a small amount of the mushroom mixture on to each leaf, top with a mint leaf and serve.

# THAI ASPARAGUS

*THIS IS AN EXCITINGLY DIFFERENT WAY OF COOKING ASPARAGUS. THE CRUNCHY TEXTURE IS RETAINED AND THE FLAVOUR IS COMPLEMENTED BY THE ADDITION OF GALANGAL AND CHILLI.*

SERVES FOUR

INGREDIENTS

350g/12oz asparagus stalks
30ml/2 tbsp vegetable oil
1 garlic clove, crushed
15ml/1 tbsp sesame seeds, toasted
2.5cm/1in piece fresh galangal, finely shredded
1 fresh red chilli, seeded and finely chopped
15ml/1 tbsp Thai fish sauce
15ml/1 tbsp light soy sauce
45ml/3 tbsp water
5ml/1 tsp palm sugar or light muscovado (brown) sugar

**VARIATIONS**
Try this with broccoli or pak choi (bok choy). The sauce also works very well with green beans.

1 Snap the asparagus stalks. They will break naturally at the junction between the woody base and the more tender portion of the stalk. Discard the woody parts of the stems.

2 Heat the oil in a wok and stir-fry the garlic, sesame seeds and galangal for 3–4 seconds, until the garlic is just beginning to turn golden.

3 Add the asparagus stalks and chilli, toss to mix, then add the fish sauce, soy sauce, water and sugar. Using two spoons, toss over the heat for a further 2 minutes, or until the asparagus just begins to soften and the liquid is reduced by half.

4 Carefully transfer to a warmed platter and serve immediately.

# STIR-FRIED SQUID WITH GINGER

*THE ABUNDANCE OF FISH AROUND THE GULF OF THAILAND SUSTAINS THRIVING MARKETS FOR THE RESTAURANT AND HOTEL TRADE, AND EVERY MARKET NATURALLY FEATURES STALLS WHERE DELICIOUS, FRESHLY-CAUGHT SEAFOOD IS COOKED AND SERVED. THIS RECIPE IS POPULAR AMONG STREET TRADERS.*

SERVES TWO

INGREDIENTS

   4 ready-prepared baby squid, total
     weight about 250g/9oz
   15ml/1 tbsp vegetable oil
   2 garlic cloves, finely chopped
   30ml/2 tbsp soy sauce
   2.5cm/1in piece fresh root ginger,
     peeled and finely chopped
   juice of ½ lemon
   5ml/1 tsp granulated sugar
   2 spring onions (scallions), chopped

**VARIATIONS**

This dish is often prepared with fresh galangal rather than ginger and works well with most kinds of seafood, including prawns (shrimp) and scallops.

**1** Rinse the squid well and pat dry with kitchen paper. Cut the bodies into rings and halve the tentacles, if necessary.

**2** Heat the oil in a wok or frying pan and cook the garlic until golden brown, but do not let it burn. Add the squid and stir-fry for 30 seconds over a high heat.

**3** Add the soy sauce, ginger, lemon juice, sugar and spring onions. Stir-fry a further 30 seconds, then serve.

**COOK'S TIP**

Squid has an undeserved reputation for being rubbery in texture. This is always a result of overcooking it.

# STIR-FRIED PRAWNS WITH NOODLES

*ONE OF THE MOST APPEALING ASPECTS OF THAI FOOD IS ITS APPEARANCE. INGREDIENTS ARE CAREFULLY CHOSEN SO THAT EACH DISH, EVEN A SIMPLE STIR-FRY LIKE THIS ONE, IS BALANCED IN TERMS OF COLOUR, TEXTURE AND FLAVOUR.*

SERVES FOUR

INGREDIENTS

   130g/4½oz rice noodles
   30ml/2 tbsp groundnut (peanut) oil
   1 large garlic clove, crushed
   150g/5oz large prawns (shrimp),
     peeled and deveined
   15g/½oz dried shrimp
   1 piece mooli (daikon), about
     75g/3oz, grated
   15ml/1 tbsp Thai fish sauce
   30ml/2 tbsp soy sauce
   30ml/2 tbsp palm sugar or light
     muscovado (brown) sugar
   30ml/2 tbsp fresh lime juice
   90g/3½oz/1¾ cups beansprouts
   40g/1½oz/⅓ cup peanuts, chopped
   15ml/1 tbsp sesame oil
   chopped coriander (cilantro),
     5ml/1 tsp dried chilli flakes and
     2 shallots, finely chopped, to garnish

**1** Soak the noodles in a bowl of boiling water for 5 minutes, or according to the packet instructions. Heat the oil in a wok or large frying pan. Add the garlic, and stir-fry over a medium heat for 2–3 minutes, until golden brown.

**2** Add the prawns, dried shrimp and grated mooli and stir-fry for a further 2 minutes. Stir in the fish sauce, soy sauce, sugar and lime juice.

**3** Drain the noodles thoroughly, then snip them into smaller lengths with scissors. Add to the wok or pan with the beansprouts, peanuts and sesame oil. Toss to mix, then stir-fry for 2 minutes. Serve immediately, garnished with the coriander, chilli flakes and shallots.

**COOK'S TIP**
Some cooks salt the mooli and leave it to drain, then rinse and dry before use.

# STIR-FRIED CHICKEN <u>WITH</u> BASIL <u>AND</u> CHILLI

*THIS QUICK AND EASY CHICKEN DISH IS AN EXCELLENT INTRODUCTION TO THAI CUISINE. IF YOU WANT A MORE PUNGENT, SPICY FLAVOUR, YOU COULD USE HOLY BASIL INSTEAD OF THAI BASIL. DEEP-FRYING THE LEAVES ADDS ANOTHER DIMENSION TO THIS DISH.*

**2** Add the pieces of chicken to the wok or pan, in batches if necessary, and stir-fry until the chicken changes colour.

**3** Stir in the fish sauce, soy sauce and sugar. Continue to stir-fry the mixture for 3–4 minutes, or until the chicken is fully cooked and golden brown.

**4** Stir in the fresh Thai basil leaves. Spoon the mixture on to a warm platter, or into individual dishes. Garnish with the chopped chillies and deep-fried Thai basil and serve immediately.

**COOK'S TIP**

To deep-fry Thai basil leaves, first make sure that the leaves are completely dry or they will splutter when added to the oil. Heat vegetable or groundnut (peanut) oil in a wok or deep-fryer to 190°C/375°F or until a cube of bread, added to the oil, browns in about 45 seconds. Add the leaves and deep-fry them briefly until they are crisp and translucent – this will take only about 30–40 seconds. Lift out the leaves using a slotted spoon or wire basket and leave them to drain on kitchen paper before using.

SERVES FOUR TO SIX

INGREDIENTS
  45ml/3 tbsp vegetable oil
  4 garlic cloves, thinly sliced
  2–4 fresh red chillies, seeded and
    finely chopped
  450g/1lb skinless boneless chicken
    breast portions, cut into
    bitesize pieces
  45ml/3 tbsp Thai fish sauce
  10ml/2 tsp dark soy sauce
  5ml/1 tsp granulated sugar
  10–12 fresh Thai basil leaves
  2 fresh red chillies, seeded and
    finely chopped, and about 20 deep-
    fried Thai basil leaves, to garnish

**1** Heat the oil in a wok or large, heavy frying pan. Add the garlic and chillies and stir-fry over a medium heat for 1–2 minutes until the garlic is golden. Take care not to let the garlic burn, otherwise it will taste bitter.

# CASHEW CHICKEN

*ALTHOUGH IT IS NOT NATIVE TO SOUTH-EAST ASIA, THE CASHEW TREE IS HIGHLY PRIZED IN THAILAND AND THE CLASSIC PARTNERSHIP OF THESE SLIGHTLY SWEET NUTS WITH CHICKEN IS IMMENSELY POPULAR BOTH IN THAILAND AND ABROAD.*

SERVES FOUR TO SIX

INGREDIENTS
  450g/1lb boneless chicken
    breast portions
  1 red (bell) pepper
  2 garlic cloves
  4 dried red chillies
  30ml/2 tbsp vegetable oil
  30ml/2 tbsp oyster sauce
  15ml/1 tbsp soy sauce
  pinch of granulated sugar
  1 bunch spring onions (scallions), cut
    into 5cm/2in lengths
  175g/6oz/1½ cups cashews, roasted
  coriander (cilantro) leaves,
    to garnish

1 Remove and discard the skin from the chicken breasts and trim off any excess fat. With a sharp knife, cut the chicken into bitesize pieces and set aside.

2 Halve the red pepper, scrape out the seeds and membranes and discard, then cut the flesh into 2cm/¾in dice. Peel and thinly slice the garlic and chop the dried red chillies.

3 Preheat a wok and then heat the oil. The best way to do this is to drizzle a "necklace" of oil around the inner rim of the wok, so that it drops down to coat the entire inner surface. Make sure the coating is even by swirling the wok.

4 Add the garlic and dried chillies to the wok and stir-fry over a medium heat until golden. Do not let the garlic burn, otherwise it will taste bitter.

5 Add the chicken to the wok and stir-fry until it is cooked through, then add the red pepper. If the mixture is very dry, add a little water.

6 Stir in the oyster sauce, soy sauce and sugar. Add the spring onions and cashew nuts. Stir-fry for 1–2 minutes more, until heated through. Spoon into a warm dish and serve immediately, garnished with the coriander leaves.

**COOK'S TIP**
The Thais not only value cashew nuts, but also the "fruit" under which each nut grows. Although they are known as cashew apples, these so-called fruits are actually bulbous portions of the stem. They may be pink, red or yellow in colour and the crisp, sweet flesh can be eaten raw or made into a refreshing drink. They have even been used for making jam. Cashew apples – and undried nuts – are rarely seen outside their growing regions.

# DUCK AND SESAME STIR-FRY

*THIS RECIPE COMES FROM NORTHERN THAILAND AND IS INTENDED FOR GAME BIRDS, AS FARMED DUCK WOULD HAVE TOO MUCH FAT. USE WILD DUCK IF YOU CAN GET IT, OR EVEN PARTRIDGE, PHEASANT OR PIGEON. IF YOU DO USE FARMED DUCK, YOU SHOULD REMOVE THE SKIN AND FAT LAYER.*

SERVES FOUR

INGREDIENTS
    250g/9oz boneless wild duck meat
    15ml/1 tbsp sesame oil
    15ml/1 tbsp vegetable oil
    4 garlic cloves, finely sliced
    2.5ml/½ tsp dried chilli flakes
    15ml/1 tbsp Thai fish sauce
    15ml/1 tbsp light soy sauce
    120ml/4fl oz/½ cup water
    1 head broccoli, cut into small florets
    coriander (cilantro) and 15ml/1 tbsp
        toasted sesame seeds, to garnish

**VARIATIONS**
Pak choi (bok choy) or Chinese flowering cabbage can be used instead of broccoli.

**1** Cut the duck meat into bitesize pieces. Heat the oils in a wok or large, heavy frying pan and stir-fry the garlic over a medium heat until it is golden brown – do not let it burn. Add the duck to the pan and stir-fry for a further 2 minutes, until the meat begins to brown.

**2** Stir in the chilli flakes, fish sauce, soy sauce and water. Add the broccoli and continue to stir-fry for about 2 minutes, until the duck is just cooked through.

**3** Serve on warmed plates, garnished with coriander and sesame seeds.

# LEMON GRASS PORK

*CHILLIES AND LEMON GRASS ARE THE MAIN FLAVOURINGS IN THIS SIMPLE STIR-FRY, WHILE PEANUTS ADD AN INTERESTING CONTRAST IN TEXTURE. THE CRUSHED BLACK PEPPERCORNS IN THE MARINADE CONTRIBUTE EXTRA SPICINESS AND HEAT TO THE DISH.*

SERVES FOUR

INGREDIENTS

    675g/1½lb boneless
      pork loin
    2 lemon grass stalks,
      finely chopped
    4 spring onions (scallions),
      thinly sliced
    5ml/1 tsp salt
    12 black peppercorns,
      coarsely crushed
    30ml/2 tbsp groundnut
      (peanut) oil
    2 garlic cloves, chopped
    2 fresh red chillies, seeded
      and chopped
    5ml/1 tsp soft light brown sugar
    30ml/2 tbsp Thai fish sauce
    25g/1oz/¼ cup roasted unsalted
      peanuts, chopped
    ground black pepper
    cooked rice noodles, to serve
    coarsely torn coriander (cilantro)
      leaves, to garnish

**1** Trim any excess fat from the pork. Cut the meat across into 5mm/¼in thick slices, then cut each slice into 5mm/¼in strips. Put the pork into a bowl with the lemon grass, spring onions, salt and crushed peppercorns; mix well. Cover with clear film (plastic wrap) and leave to marinate in a cool place for 30 minutes.

**2** Preheat a wok, add the oil and swirl it around. Add the pork mixture and stir-fry over a medium heat for about 3 minutes, until browned all over.

**3** Add the garlic and red chillies and stir-fry for a further 5–8 minutes over a medium heat, until the pork is cooked through and tender.

**4** Add the sugar, fish sauce and chopped peanuts and toss to mix, then season to taste with black pepper. Serve immediately on a bed of rice noodles, garnished with the coarsely torn coriander leaves.

**COOK'S TIP**
The heat in chillies is not in the seeds, but in the membranes surrounding them, which are removed along with the seeds.

# SWEET *AND* SOUR PORK, THAI-STYLE

*IT WAS THE CHINESE WHO ORIGINALLY CREATED SWEET AND SOUR COOKING, BUT THE THAIS ALSO DO IT VERY WELL. THIS VERSION HAS A FRESHER AND CLEANER FLAVOUR THAN THE ORIGINAL. IT MAKES A GOOD ONE-DISH MEAL WHEN SERVED OVER RICE.*

SERVES FOUR

INGREDIENTS

350g/12oz lean pork
30ml/2 tbsp vegetable oil
4 garlic cloves, thinly sliced
1 small red onion, sliced
30ml/2 tbsp Thai fish sauce
15ml/1 tbsp granulated sugar
1 red (bell) pepper, seeded and diced
½ cucumber, seeded and sliced
2 plum tomatoes, cut into wedges
115g/4oz piece of fresh pineapple, cut into small chunks
2 spring onions (scallions), cut into short lengths
ground black pepper
To garnish
coriander (cilantro) leaves
spring onions (scallions), shredded

**1** Place the pork in the freezer for 30–40 minutes, until firm. Using a sharp knife, cut it into thin strips.

**2** Heat the oil in a wok or large frying pan. Add the garlic. Cook over a medium heat until golden, then add the pork and stir-fry for 4–5 minutes. Add the onion slices and toss to mix.

**3** Add the fish sauce, sugar and ground black pepper to taste. Toss the mixture over the heat for 3–4 minutes more.

**4** Stir in the red pepper, cucumber, tomatoes, pineapple and spring onions. Stir-fry for 3–4 minutes more, then spoon into a bowl. Garnish with the coriander and spring onions and serve.

# STIR-FRIED BEEF IN OYSTER SAUCE

*ANOTHER SIMPLE BUT DELICIOUS RECIPE. IN THAILAND THIS IS OFTEN MADE WITH JUST STRAW MUSHROOMS, WHICH ARE READILY AVAILABLE FRESH, BUT OYSTER MUSHROOMS MAKE A GOOD SUBSTITUTE AND USING A MIXTURE MAKES THE DISH EXTRA INTERESTING.*

SERVES FOUR TO SIX

INGREDIENTS
  450g/1lb rump (round) steak
  30ml/2 tbsp soy sauce
  15ml/1 tbsp cornflour (cornstarch)
  45ml/3 tbsp vegetable oil
  15ml/1 tbsp chopped garlic
  15ml/1 tbsp chopped fresh
    root ginger
  225g/8oz/3¼ cups mixed mushrooms
    such as shiitake, oyster and straw
  30ml/2 tbsp oyster sauce
  5ml/1 tsp granulated sugar
  4 spring onions (scallions), cut into
    short lengths
  ground black pepper
  2 fresh red chillies, seeded and cut
    into strips, to garnish

**1** Place the steak in the freezer for 30–40 minutes, until firm, then, using a sharp knife, slice it on the diagonal into long thin strips.

**2** Mix together the soy sauce and cornflour in a large bowl. Add the steak, turning to coat well, cover with clear film (plastic wrap) and leave to marinate at room temperature for 1–2 hours.

**3** Heat half the oil in a wok or large, heavy frying pan. Add the garlic and ginger and cook for 1–2 minutes, until fragrant. Drain the steak, add it to the wok or pan and stir well to separate the strips. Cook, stirring frequently, for a further 1–2 minutes, until the steak is browned all over and tender. Remove from the wok or pan and set aside.

**4** Heat the remaining oil in the wok or pan. Add the shiitake, oyster and straw mushrooms. Stir-fry over a medium heat until golden brown.

**5** Return the steak to the wok and mix it with the mushrooms. Spoon in the oyster sauce and sugar, mix well, then add ground black pepper to taste. Toss over the heat until all the ingredients are thoroughly combined.

**6** Stir in the spring onions. Tip the mixture on to a serving platter, garnish with the strips of red chilli and serve.

# RICE AND NOODLE DISHES

Thai fragrant rice, also known as jasmine rice, is valued the world over for its subtle fragrance. It goes well with both savoury and sweet dishes and is particularly delicious when cooked in coconut milk or served with toasted coconut strips. Most noodles are made from rice, and are served as an accompaniment to main meals or mixed with other ingredients to make a complete dish. Sometimes they are simply served plain, with a selection of condiments or dips.

# COCONUT RICE

*THIS RICH DISH IS USUALLY SERVED WITH A TANGY PAPAYA SALAD TO BALANCE THE SWEETNESS OF THE COCONUT MILK AND SUGAR. IT IS ONE OF THOSE COMFORTING TREATS THAT EVERYONE ENJOYS.*

SERVES FOUR TO SIX

INGREDIENTS
    250ml/8fl oz/1 cup water
    475ml/16fl oz/2 cups coconut milk
    2.5ml/½ tsp salt
    30ml/2 tbsp granulated sugar
    450g/1lb/2⅔ cups jasmine rice

**COOK'S TIP**
For a special occasion serve in a halved papaya and garnish with thin shreds of fresh coconut. Use a vegetable peeler to pare the coconut finely, as you would when making curls of Parmesan cheese.

**1** Place the measured water, coconut milk, salt and sugar in a heavy pan. Wash the rice in several changes of cold water until it runs clear.

**2** Add the jasmine rice, cover tightly with a lid and bring to the boil over a medium heat. Reduce the heat to low and simmer gently, without lifting the lid unnecessarily, for 15–20 minutes, until the rice is tender and cooked through. Test it by biting a grain.

**3** Turn off the heat and leave the rice to rest in the pan, still covered with the lid, for a further 5–10 minutes.

**4** Gently fluff up the rice grains with chopsticks or a fork before transferring it to a warmed dish and serving.

# FRIED JASMINE RICE WITH PRAWNS AND HOLY BASIL

*HOLY BASIL (BAI GRAPAO) HAS A UNIQUE, PUNGENT FLAVOUR THAT IS BOTH SPICY AND SHARP. IT CAN BE FOUND IN MOST ASIAN FOOD MARKETS.*

SERVES FOUR TO SIX

INGREDIENTS

   45ml/3 tbsp vegetable oil
   1 egg, beaten
   1 onion, chopped
   15ml/1 tbsp chopped garlic
   15ml/1 tbsp shrimp paste
   1kg/2¼lb/4 cups cooked jasmine rice
   350g/12oz cooked shelled prawns
    (shrimp)
   50g/2oz thawed frozen peas
   oyster sauce, to taste
   2 spring onions (scallions), chopped
   15–20 holy basil leaves, roughly
    snipped, plus an extra sprig,
    to garnish

**1** Heat 15ml/1 tbsp of the oil in a wok or frying pan. Add the beaten egg and swirl it around to set like a thin pancake.

**2** Cook the pancake (on one side only) over a gentle heat until golden. Slide the pancake on to a board, roll up and cut into thin strips. Set aside.

**3** Heat the remaining oil in the wok or pan, add the onion and garlic and stir-fry for 2–3 minutes. Stir in the shrimp paste and mix well until thoroughly combined.

**4** Add the rice, prawns and peas and toss and stir together, until everything is heated through.

**5** Season with oyster sauce to taste, taking great care as the shrimp paste is salty. Mix in the spring onions and basil leaves. Transfer to a serving dish and top with the strips of egg pancake. Serve, garnished with a sprig of basil.

# FRIED RICE WITH PORK

*THIS CLASSIC RICE DISH LOOKS PARTICULARLY PRETTY GARNISHED WITH STRIPS OF OMELETTE, AS IN THE RECIPE FOR FRIED JASMINE RICE WITH PRAWNS AND HOLY BASIL.*

SERVES FOUR TO SIX

INGREDIENTS
  45ml/3 tbsp vegetable oil
  1 onion, chopped
  15ml/1 tbsp chopped garlic
  115g/4oz pork, cut into small cubes
  2 eggs, beaten
  1kg/2¼lb/4 cups cooked rice
  30ml/2 tbsp Thai fish sauce
  15ml/1 tbsp dark soy sauce
  2.5ml/½ tsp caster (superfine) sugar
  4 spring onions (scallions),
    finely sliced, to garnish
  2 red chillies, sliced, to garnish
  1 lime, cut into wedges, to garnish

**COOK'S TIP**
To make 1kg/2¼lb/4 cups cooked rice, you will need approximately 400g/14oz/ 2 cups uncooked rice.

**1** Heat the oil in a wok or large frying pan. Add the onion and garlic and cook for about 2 minutes until softened.

**2** Add the pork to the softened onion and garlic. Stir-fry until the pork changes colour and is cooked.

**3** Add the eggs and cook until scrambled into small lumps.

**4** Add the rice and continue to stir and toss, to coat it with the oil and prevent it from sticking.

**5** Add the fish sauce, soy sauce and sugar and mix well. Continue to fry until the rice is thoroughly heated. Spoon into warmed individual bowls and serve, garnished with sliced spring onions, chillies and lime wedges.

# FRIED RICE WITH BEEF

*ONE OF THE JOYS OF THAI COOKING IS THE EASE AND SPEED WITH WHICH A REALLY GOOD MEAL CAN BE PREPARED. THIS ONE CAN BE ON THE TABLE IN 15 MINUTES.*

SERVES FOUR

INGREDIENTS
200g/7oz beef steak
15ml/1 tbsp vegetable oil
2 garlic cloves,
   finely chopped
1 egg
250g/9oz/2¼ cups cooked
   jasmine rice
½ medium head broccoli,
   coarsely chopped
30ml/2 tbsp dark soy sauce
15ml/1 tbsp light soy sauce
5ml/1 tsp palm sugar or light
   muscovado (brown) sugar
15ml/1 tbsp Thai fish sauce
ground black pepper
chilli sauce, to serve

**1** Trim the steak and cut into very thin strips with a sharp knife.

**2** Heat the oil in a wok or frying pan and cook the garlic over a low to medium heat until golden. Do not let it burn. Increase the heat to high, add the steak and stir-fry for 2 minutes.

**3** Move the pieces of beef to the edges of the wok or pan and break the egg into the centre. When the egg starts to set, stir-fry it with the meat.

**4** Add the rice and toss all the contents of the wok together, scraping up any residue on the base, then add the broccoli, soy sauces, sugar and fish sauce and stir-fry for 2 minutes more. Season to taste with pepper and serve immediately with chilli sauce.

**COOK'S TIP**
Soy sauce is made from fermented soya beans. The first extraction is sold as light soy sauce and has a delicate, "beany" fragrance. Dark soy sauce has been allowed to mature for longer.

# PLAIN NOODLES WITH FOUR FLAVOURS

*A WONDERFULLY SIMPLE WAY OF SERVING NOODLES, THIS DISH ALLOWS EACH INDIVIDUAL DINER TO SEASON THEIR OWN, SPRINKLING OVER THE FOUR FLAVOURS AS THEY LIKE. FLAVOURINGS ARE ALWAYS PUT OUT IN LITTLE BOWLS WHENEVER NOODLES ARE SERVED.*

### SERVES FOUR

### INGREDIENTS
    4 small fresh red or green chillies
    60ml/4 tbsp Thai fish sauce
    60ml/4 tbsp rice vinegar
    granulated sugar
    mild or hot chilli powder
    350g/12oz fresh or dried noodles

**1** Prepare the four flavours. For the first, finely chop 2 small red or green chillies, discarding the seeds or leaving them in, depending on how hot you like your flavouring. Place them in a small bowl and add the Thai fish sauce.

**2** For the second flavour, chop the remaining chillies finely and mix them with the rice vinegar in a small bowl. Put the sugar and chilli powder in separate small bowls.

**3** Cook the noodles until tender, following the instructions on the packet. Drain well, tip into a large bowl and serve immediately with the four flavours handed separately.

# THAI NOODLES <u>WITH</u> CHINESE CHIVES

*THIS RECIPE REQUIRES A LITTLE TIME FOR PREPARATION, BUT THE COOKING TIME IS VERY FAST. EVERYTHING IS COOKED IN A HOT WOK AND SHOULD BE EATEN IMMEDIATELY. THIS IS A FILLING AND TASTY VEGETARIAN DISH, IDEAL FOR A WEEKEND LUNCH.*

SERVES FOUR

INGREDIENTS
    350g/12oz dried rice noodles
    1cm/½in piece fresh root ginger,
      peeled and grated
    30ml/2 tbsp light soy sauce
    45ml/3 tbsp vegetable oil
    225g/8oz Quorn (mycoprotein), cut
      into small cubes
    2 garlic cloves, crushed
    1 large onion, cut into thin wedges
    115g/4oz fried tofu, thinly sliced
    1 fresh green chilli, seeded and
      thinly sliced
    175g/6oz/2 cups beansprouts
    2 large bunches garlic chives, total
      weight about 115g/4oz, cut into
      5cm/2in lengths
    50g/2oz/½ cup roasted
      peanuts, ground
    30ml/2 tbsp dark soy sauce
    30ml/2 tbsp chopped fresh coriander
      (cilantro), and 1 lemon, cut into
      wedges, to garnish

**1** Place the noodles in a bowl, cover with warm water and leave to soak for 30 minutes. Drain and set aside.

**2** Mix the ginger, light soy sauce and 15ml/1 tbsp of the oil in a bowl. Add the Quorn, then set aside for 10 minutes. Drain, reserving the marinade.

**3** Heat 15ml/1 tbsp of the remaining oil in a frying pan and cook the garlic for a few seconds. Add the Quorn and stir-fry for 3–4 minutes. Using a slotted spoon, transfer to a plate and set aside.

**4** Heat the remaining oil in the pan and stir-fry the onion for 3–4 minutes, until softened and tinged with brown. Add the tofu and chilli, stir-fry briefly and then add the noodles. Stir-fry over a medium heat for 4–5 minutes.

**5** Stir in the beansprouts, garlic chives and most of the ground peanuts, reserving a little for the garnish. Stir well, then add the Quorn, the dark soy sauce and the reserved marinade.

**6** When hot, spoon on to serving plates and garnish with the remaining ground peanuts, the coriander and lemon.

# NOODLES AND VEGETABLES IN COCONUT SAUCE

*WHEN EVERYDAY VEGETABLES ARE GIVEN THE THAI TREATMENT, THE RESULT IS A DELECTABLE DISH WHICH EVERYONE WILL ENJOY. NOODLES ADD BULK AND A WELCOME CONTRAST IN TEXTURE.*

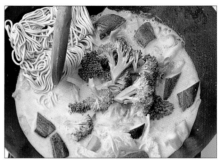

**3** Increase the heat to medium, stir in the coconut milk and vegetable stock and bring to the boil. Add the broccoli florets and the noodles, lower the heat and simmer gently for 20 minutes.

**4** Meanwhile, make the garnish. Split the lemon grass stalks lengthways through the root. Gather the coriander into a small bouquet and lay it on a platter, following the curve of the rim.

**5** Tuck the lemon grass halves into the coriander bouquet and add the chillies to resemble flowers.

**6** Stir the fish sauce, soy sauce and chopped coriander into the noodle mixture. Spoon on to the platter, taking care not to disturb the herb bouquet, and serve immediately.

SERVES FOUR TO SIX

INGREDIENTS
   30ml/2 tbsp sunflower oil
   1 lemon grass stalk, finely chopped
   15ml/1 tbsp Thai red curry paste
   1 onion, thickly sliced
   3 courgettes (zucchini), thickly sliced
   115g/4oz Savoy cabbage,
     thickly sliced
   2 carrots, thickly sliced
   150g/5oz broccoli, stem thickly
     sliced and head separated
     into florets
   2 × 400ml/14fl oz cans coconut milk
   475ml/16fl oz/2 cups vegetable stock
   150g/5oz dried egg noodles
   15ml/1 tbsp Thai fish sauce
   30ml/2 tbsp soy sauce
   60ml/4 tbsp chopped fresh
     coriander (cilantro)
For the garnish
   2 lemon grass stalks
   1 bunch fresh coriander (cilantro)
   8–10 small fresh red chillies

**1** Heat the oil in a large pan or wok. Add the lemon grass and red curry paste and stir-fry for 2–3 seconds. Add the onion and cook over a medium heat, stirring occasionally, for about 5–10 minutes, until the onion has softened but not browned.

**2** Add the courgettes, cabbage, carrots and slices of broccoli stem. Using two spoons, toss the vegetables with the onion mixture. Reduce the heat to low and cook gently, stirring occasionally, for a further 5 minutes.

# SWEET AND HOT VEGETABLE NOODLES

*THIS NOODLE DISH HAS ONLY THE MILDEST SUGGESTION OF HEAT. GINGER AND PLUM SAUCE GIVE IT ITS FRUITY FLAVOUR, WHILE LIME ADDS A DELICIOUS TANG.*

### SERVES FOUR

### INGREDIENTS

130g/4½oz dried rice noodles
30ml/2 tbsp groundnut (peanut) oil
2.5cm/1in piece fresh root ginger,
  sliced into thin batons
1 garlic clove, crushed
130g/4½oz drained canned bamboo
  shoots, sliced into thin batons
2 medium carrots, sliced into batons
130g/4½oz/1½ cups beansprouts
1 small white cabbage, shredded
30ml/2 tbsp Thai fish sauce
30ml/2 tbsp soy sauce
30ml/2 tbsp plum sauce
10ml/2 tsp sesame oil
15ml/1 tbsp palm sugar or light
  muscovado (brown) sugar
juice of ½ lime
90g/3½oz mooli (daikon), sliced into
  thin batons
small bunch fresh coriander
  (cilantro), chopped
60ml/4 tbsp sesame seeds, toasted

**1** Cook the noodles in a large pan of boiling water, following the instructions on the packet. Meanwhile, heat the oil in a wok or large frying pan and stir-fry the ginger and garlic for 2–3 minutes over a medium heat, until golden.

**2** Drain the noodles and set them aside. Add the bamboo shoots to the wok, increase the heat to high and stir-fry for 5 minutes. Add the carrots, beansprouts and cabbage and stir-fry for a further 5 minutes, until they are beginning to char on the edges.

**3** Stir in the sauces, sesame oil, sugar and lime juice. Add the mooli and coriander, toss to mix, then spoon into a warmed bowl, sprinkle with toasted sesame seeds and serve immediately.

**COOK'S TIP**
Use a large, sharp knife for shredding cabbage. Remove any tough outer leaves, if necessary, then cut the cabbage into quarters. Cut off and discard the hard core from each quarter, place flat side down, then slice the cabbage very thinly to make fine shreds.

# CELLOPHANE NOODLES WITH PORK

*SIMPLE, SPEEDY AND SATISFYING, THIS IS AN EXCELLENT WAY OF USING MUNG BEAN NOODLES. THE DISH IS POPULAR ALL OVER THAILAND.*

SERVES TWO

INGREDIENTS
    200g/7oz cellophane noodles
    30ml/2 tbsp vegetable oil
    15ml/1 tbsp magic paste
    200g/7oz minced (ground) pork
    1 fresh green or red chilli, seeded
      and finely chopped
    300g/11oz/3½ cups beansprouts
    bunch spring onions (scallions),
      finely chopped
    30ml/2 tbsp soy sauce
    30ml/2 tbsp Thai fish sauce
    30ml/2 tbsp sweet chilli sauce
    15ml/1 tbsp palm sugar or light
      muscovado (brown) sugar
    30ml/2 tbsp rice vinegar
    30ml/2 tbsp roasted peanuts,
      chopped, to garnish
    small bunch fresh coriander
      (cilantro), chopped, to garnish

**1** Place the noodles in a large bowl, cover with boiling water and soak for 10 minutes. Drain the noodles and set aside until ready to use.

**2** Heat the oil in a wok or large, heavy frying pan. Add the magic paste and stir-fry for 2–3 seconds, then add the pork. Stir-fry the meat, breaking it up with a wooden spatula, for 2–3 minutes, until browned all over.

**3** Add the chopped chilli to the meat and stir-fry for 3–4 seconds, then add the beansprouts and chopped spring onions, stir-frying for a few seconds after each addition.

**4** Snip the noodles into 5cm/2in lengths and add to the wok, with the soy sauce, Thai fish sauce, sweet chilli sauce, sugar and rice vinegar.

**5** Toss the ingredients together over the heat until well combined and the noodles have warmed through. Pile on to a platter or into a large bowl. Sprinkle over the peanuts and coriander and serve immediately.

**VARIATION**
This dish is also very good made with chicken. Replace the pork with the same quantity of minced (ground) chicken.

# SPICY FRIED NOODLES

*THIS IS A WONDERFULLY VERSATILE DISH AS YOU CAN ADAPT IT TO INCLUDE YOUR FAVOURITE INGREDIENTS — JUST AS LONG AS YOU KEEP A BALANCE OF FLAVOURS, TEXTURES AND COLOURS.*

SERVES FOUR

INGREDIENTS

225g/8oz egg thread noodles
60ml/4 tbsp vegetable oil
2 garlic cloves, finely chopped
175g/6oz pork fillet (tenderloin),
   sliced into thin strips
1 skinless, boneless chicken breast
   portion (about 175g/6oz), sliced
   into thin strips
115g/4oz/1 cup cooked peeled
   prawns (shrimp), rinsed if canned
45ml/3 tbsp fresh lemon juice
45ml/3 tbsp Thai fish sauce
30ml/2 tbsp soft light brown sugar
2 eggs, beaten
½ fresh red chilli, seeded and
   finely chopped
50g/2oz/⅔ cup beansprouts
60ml/4 tbsp roasted
   peanuts, chopped
3 spring onions (scallions), cut into
   5cm/2in lengths and shredded
45ml/3 tbsp chopped fresh
   coriander (cilantro)

**1** Bring a large pan of water to the boil. Add the noodles, remove the pan from the heat and leave for 5 minutes.

**2** Meanwhile, heat 45ml/3 tbsp of the oil in a wok or large frying pan, add the garlic and cook for 30 seconds. Add the pork and chicken and stir-fry until lightly browned, then add the prawns and stir-fry for 2 minutes.

**3** Stir in the lemon juice, then add the fish sauce and sugar. Stir-fry until the sugar has dissolved.

**4** Drain the noodles and add to the wok or pan with the remaining 15ml/1 tbsp oil. Toss all the ingredients together.

**5** Pour the beaten eggs over the noodles and stir-fry until almost set, then add the chilli and beansprouts.

**6** Divide the roasted peanuts, spring onions and coriander leaves into two equal portions, add one portion to the pan and stir-fry for about 2 minutes.

**7** Tip the noodles on to a serving platter. Sprinkle on the remaining roasted peanuts, spring onions and chopped coriander and serve immediately.

**COOK'S TIP**
Store beansprouts in the refrigerator and use within a day of purchase, as they tend to lose their crispness and become slimy and unpleasant quite quickly. The most commonly used beansprouts are sprouted mung beans, but you could use other types of beansprouts instead.

# CHIANG MAI NOODLES

*AN INTERESTING NOODLE DISH THAT COMBINES SOFT, BOILED NOODLES WITH CRISP DEEP-FRIED ONES AND ADDS THE USUAL PANOPLY OF THAI SWEET, HOT AND SOUR FLAVOURS.*

SERVES FOUR

INGREDIENTS

250ml/8fl oz/1 cup coconut cream
15ml/1 tbsp magic paste
5ml/1 tsp Thai red curry paste
450g/1lb chicken thigh meat,
   chopped into small pieces
30ml/2 tbsp dark soy sauce
2 red (bell) peppers, seeded and
   finely diced
600ml/1 pint/2½ cups chicken or
   vegetable stock
90g/3½oz fresh or dried rice noodles
For the garnishes
   vegetable oil, for deep-frying
   90g/3½oz fine dried rice noodles
   2 pickled garlic cloves, chopped
   small bunch fresh coriander
      (cilantro), chopped
   2 limes, cut into wedges

1 Pour the coconut cream into a large wok or frying pan and bring to the boil over a medium heat. Continue to boil, stirring frequently, for 8–10 minutes, until the milk separates and an oily sheen appears on the surface.

2 Add the magic paste and red curry paste and cook, stirring constantly, for 3–5 seconds, until fragrant.

3 Add the chicken and toss over the heat until sealed on all sides. Stir in the soy sauce and the diced peppers and stir-fry for 3–4 minutes. Pour in the stock. Bring to the boil, then lower the heat and simmer for 10–15 minutes, until the chicken is fully cooked.

4 Meanwhile, make the noodle garnish. Heat the oil in a pan or deep-fryer to 190°C/375°F or until a cube of bread, added to the oil, browns in 45 seconds. Break all the noodles in half, then divide them into four portions. Add one portion at a time to the hot oil. They will puff up on contact. As soon as they are crisp, lift the noodles out with a slotted spoon and drain on kitchen paper.

5 Bring a large pan of water to the boil and cook the fresh or dried noodles until tender, following the instructions on the packet. Drain well, divide among four warmed individual dishes, then spoon the curry sauce over them. Top each portion with a cluster of fried noodles. Sprinkle the chopped pickled garlic and coriander over the top and serve immediately, offering lime wedges for squeezing.

**COOK'S TIP**
If you are planning to serve this dish to guests, you can save on preparation time by making the noodle garnish in advance. Deep-fry the noodles a few hours before you need them and drain well on kitchen paper. Transfer the crispy noodles to a wire rack lined with fresh sheets of kitchen paper and set aside until ready to use.

# SOUTHERN CURRIED NOODLES

*CHICKEN OR PORK CAN BE USED TO PROVIDE THE PROTEIN IN THIS TASTY DISH. IT IS SO QUICK AND EASY TO PREPARE AND COOK, IT MAKES THE PERFECT SNACK FOR BUSY PEOPLE.*

SERVES TWO

INGREDIENTS

30ml/2 tbsp vegetable oil
10ml/2 tsp magic paste
1 lemon grass stalk, finely chopped
5ml/1 tsp Thai red curry paste
90g/3½oz skinless, boneless chicken
  breast portion or pork fillet
  (tenderloin), sliced into slivers
30ml/2 tbsp light soy sauce
400ml/14fl oz/1⅔ cups coconut milk
2 kaffir lime leaves, rolled into
  cylinders and thinly sliced
250g/9oz dried medium egg noodles
90g/3½oz Chinese leaves (Chinese
  cabbage), shredded
90g/3½oz spinach or watercress
  (leaves), shredded
juice of 1 lime
small bunch fresh coriander
  (cilantro), chopped

**1** Heat the oil in a wok or large, heavy frying pan. Add the magic paste and lemon grass and stir-fry over a low to medium heat for 4–5 seconds, until they give off their aroma.

**2** Stir in the curry paste, then add the chicken or pork. Stir-fry over a medium to high heat for 2 minutes, until the chicken or pork is coated in the paste and seared on all sides.

**3** Add the soy sauce, coconut milk and sliced lime leaves. Bring to a simmer, then add the noodles. Simmer gently for 4 minutes, tossing the mixture occasionally to make sure that the noodles cook evenly.

**4** Add the Chinese leaves and the watercress. Stir well, then add the lime juice. Spoon into a warmed bowl, sprinkle with the coriander and serve.

# DESSERTS

After a spicy Thai meal, it is customary to serve a platter of
fresh fruits, often carved into the most beautiful shapes, to
cleanse the palate. However, Thais also love sticky sweetmeats,
and will often pick up their favourite treats from a stall at a
night market, where they will be presented prettily on palm
leaves or with a decoration of tiny flowers. Fried bananas and
pineapple are also widely enjoyed, and these are simple to make
at home as a delicious dessert to end your meal.

# PAPAYAS IN JASMINE FLOWER SYRUP

*THE FRAGRANT SYRUP CAN BE PREPARED IN ADVANCE, USING FRESH JASMINE FLOWERS FROM A HOUSE PLANT OR THE GARDEN. IT TASTES FABULOUS WITH PAPAYAS, BUT IT IS ALSO GOOD WITH ALL SORTS OF DESSERTS. TRY IT WITH ICE CREAM OR SPOONED OVER LYCHEES OR MANGOES.*

SERVES TWO

INGREDIENTS

    105ml/7 tbsp water
    45ml/3 tbsp palm sugar or light
      muscovado (brown) sugar
    20–30 jasmine flowers, plus a
      few extra, to decorate (optional)
    2 ripe papayas
    juice of 1 lime

**COOK'S TIP**

Although scented white jasmine flowers are perfectly safe to eat, it is important to be sure that they have not been sprayed with pesticides or other harmful chemicals. Washing them may not remove all the residue.

**1** Place the water and sugar in a small pan. Heat gently, stirring occasionally, until the sugar has dissolved, then simmer, without stirring, over a low heat for 4 minutes.

**2** Pour into a bowl, leave to cool slightly, then add the jasmine flowers. Leave to steep for at least 20 minutes.

**3** Peel the papayas and slice in half lengthways. Scoop out and discard the seeds. Place the papayas on serving plates and squeeze over the lime.

**4** Strain the syrup into a clean bowl, discarding the flowers. Spoon the syrup over the papayas. If you like, decorate with a few fresh jasmine flowers.

# MANGO AND LIME FOOL

*CANNED MANGOES ARE USED HERE FOR CONVENIENCE, BUT THE DISH TASTES EVEN BETTER IF MADE WITH FRESH ONES. CHOOSE A VARIETY LIKE THE VOLUPTUOUS ALPHONSO MANGO, WHICH IS WONDERFULLY FRAGRANT AND TASTES INDESCRIBABLY DELICIOUS.*

SERVES FOUR

INGREDIENTS
   400g/14oz can sliced mango
   grated rind of 1 lime
   juice of ½ lime
   150ml/¼ pint/⅔ cup double
     (heavy) cream
   90ml/6 tbsp Greek (US strained
     plain) yogurt
   fresh mango slices, to decorate
     (optional)

**COOK'S TIP**
When mixing the cream and yogurt mixture with the mango purée, whisk just enough to combine, so as not to lose the lightness of the whipped cream mixture. If you prefer, fold the mixtures together lightly, so that the fool is rippled.

**1** Drain the canned mango slices and put them in the bowl of a food processor. Add the grated lime rind and the lime juice. Process until the mixture forms a smooth purée. Alternatively, mash the mango slices with a potato masher, then press through a sieve into a bowl with the back of a wooden spoon. Stir in the lime rind and juice.

**2** Pour the cream into a bowl and add the yogurt. Whisk until the mixture is thick and then quickly whisk in the mango mixture.

**3** Spoon into four tall cups or glasses and chill for 1–2 hours. Just before serving, decorate each glass with fresh mango slices, if you like.

# THAI FRIED PINEAPPLE

*A VERY SIMPLE AND QUICK THAI DESSERT – PINEAPPLE FRIED IN BUTTER, BROWN SUGAR AND LIME JUICE, AND SPRINKLED WITH TOASTED COCONUT. THE SLIGHTLY SHARP TASTE OF THE FRUIT MAKES THIS A VERY REFRESHING TREAT AT THE END OF A MEAL.*

**3** Meanwhile, dry-fry the coconut in a small frying pan until lightly browned. Remove from the heat and set aside.

**4** Sprinkle the sugar into the pan with the pineapple, add the lime juice and cook, stirring constantly, until the sugar has dissolved. Divide the pineapple wedges among four bowls, sprinkle with the coconut, decorate with the lime slices and serve with the yogurt.

SERVES FOUR

INGREDIENTS
  1 pineapple
  40g/1½oz/3 tbsp butter
  15ml/1 tbsp desiccated (dry
    unsweetened shredded) coconut
  60ml/4 tbsp soft light brown sugar
  60ml/4 tbsp fresh lime juice
  lime slices, to decorate
  thick and creamy natural (plain)
    yogurt, to serve

**1** Using a sharp knife, cut the top off the pineapple and peel off the skin, taking care to remove the eyes. Cut the pineapple in half and remove and discard the woody core. Cut the flesh lengthways into 1cm/½in wedges.

**2** Heat the butter in a large, heavy frying pan or wok. When it has melted, add the pineapple wedges and cook over a medium heat for 1–2 minutes on each side, or until they have turned pale golden in colour.

# FRIED BANANAS

*THESE DELICIOUSLY SWEET TREATS ARE A FAVOURITE WITH CHILDREN AND ADULTS ALIKE. IN THAILAND, YOU WILL FIND THEM ON SALE FROM PORTABLE ROADSIDE STALLS AND MARKETS AT ALMOST EVERY HOUR OF THE DAY AND NIGHT.*

SERVES FOUR

INGREDIENTS

115g/4oz/1 cup plain (all-
　purpose) flour
2.5ml/½ tsp bicarbonate of soda
　(baking soda)
pinch of salt
30ml/2 tbsp granulated sugar
1 egg, beaten
90ml/6 tbsp water
30ml/2 tbsp shredded coconut or
　15ml/1 tbsp sesame seeds
4 firm bananas
vegetable oil, for deep-frying
fresh mint sprigs, to decorate
30ml/2 tbsp clear honey, to
　serve (optional)

**4** Heat the oil in a wok or deep-fryer to a temperature of 190°C/375°F or until a cube of bread, dropped in the oil, browns in about 45 seconds. Dip the banana pieces in the batter, then gently drop a few into the oil. Deep-fry until golden brown, then lift out and drain well on kitchen paper.

**5** Cook the remaining banana pieces in the same way. Serve immediately with honey, if using, and decorated with sprigs of fresh mint.

**1** Sift the flour, bicarbonate of soda and salt into a large bowl. Stir in the granulated sugar and the egg, and whisk in just enough of the water to make quite a thin batter.

**2** Whisk the shredded coconut or sesame seeds into the batter so that they are evenly distributed.

**3** Peel the bananas. Carefully cut each one in half lengthways, then in half crossways to make 16 pieces of about the same size. Don't do this until you are ready to cook them because, once peeled, bananas quickly discolour.

**VARIATIONS**
This recipe works just as well with many other types of fruit, such as pineapple rings or apple wedges.

# STEAMED CUSTARD IN NECTARINES

*STEAMING NECTARINES OR PEACHES BRINGS OUT THEIR NATURAL COLOUR AND SWEETNESS, SO THIS IS A GOOD WAY OF MAKING THE MOST OF UNDERRIPE OR LESS FLAVOURFUL FRUIT.*

### SERVES FOUR TO SIX

INGREDIENTS
6 nectarines
1 large (US extra large) egg
45ml/3 tbsp palm sugar or light
muscovado (brown) sugar
30ml/2 tbsp coconut milk

**COOK'S TIP**
Palm sugar, also known as jaggery, is made from the sap of certain Asian palm trees, such as coconut and palmyrah. It is available from Asian food stores. If you buy it as a cake or large lump, grate it before use.

**1** Cut the nectarines in half. Using a teaspoon, scoop out the stones (pits) and a little of the surrounding flesh.

**2** Lightly beat the egg, then add the sugar and the coconut milk. Beat until the sugar has dissolved.

**3** Transfer the nectarines to a steamer and carefully fill the cavities three-quarters full with the custard mixture. Steam over a pan of simmering water for 5–10 minutes. Remove from the heat and leave to cool completely before transferring to plates and serving.

# COCONUT PANCAKES

*THESE LIGHT AND SWEET PANCAKES ARE OFTEN SERVED AS STREET FOOD BY THE HAWKERS IN BANGKOK AND THEY MAKE A DELIGHTFUL DESSERT.*

MAKES EIGHT

INGREDIENTS
　75g/3oz/¾ cup plain (all-purpose)
　　flour, sifted
　60ml/4 tbsp rice flour
　45ml/3 tbsp caster (superfine) sugar
　50g/2oz/⅔ cup desiccated (dry
　　unsweetened shredded) coconut
　1 egg
　275ml/9fl oz/generous 1 cup
　　coconut milk
　vegetable oil, for frying
　lime wedges and maple syrup,
　　to serve

**1** Place the plain flour, rice flour, sugar and coconut in a bowl, stir to mix and then make a small well in the centre. Break the egg into the well and pour in the coconut milk.

**2** With a whisk or fork, beat the egg into the coconut milk and then gradually incorporate the surrounding dry ingredients, whisking constantly until the mixture forms a batter. The mixture will not be entirely smooth, because of the coconut, but there shouldn't be any large lumps.

**COOK'S TIP**
Maple syrup is not, of course, indigenous to Thailand, but then nor are chillies. It is an international favourite for serving with pancakes. Make sure that you buy the pure syrup for the best flavour.

**VARIATION**
Serve with honey instead of maple syrup, if you like.

**3** Heat a little oil in a 13cm/5in non-stick frying pan. Pour in about 45ml/ 3 tbsp of the mixture and quickly spread to a thin layer with the back of a spoon. Cook over a high heat for about 30–60 seconds, until bubbles appear on the surface of the pancake, then turn it over with a spatula and cook the other side until golden.

**4** Slide the pancake on to a plate and keep it warm in a very low oven. Make more pancakes in the same way. Serve warm with lime wedges for squeezing and maple syrup for drizzling.

# FOOD AND SHOPPING

## AUSTRALIA

Asian Supermarkets Pty Ltd
116 Charters Towers Road
Townsville QLD 4810
Tel: (07) 4772 3997
Fax: (07) 4771 3919

Kongs Trading Pty Ltd
8 Kingscote Street
Kewdale WA 6105
Tel: (08) 9353 3380
Fax: (08) 9353 3390

Duc Hung Long Asian Foodstore
95 The Crescent
Fairfield NSW 2165
Tel: (02) 9728 1092

Exotic Asian Groceries Q
Supercentre
Cnr Market and Bermuda
  Streets
Mermaid Waters QLD 4218
Tel: (07) 5572 8188

Saigon Asian Food Retail
  and Wholesale
6 Cape Street
Dickson ACT 2602
Tel: (02) 6247 4251

The Spice and Herb Asian Shop
200 Old Cleveland Road
Capalaba QLD 4157
Tel: (07) 3245 5300

Sydney Fish Market Pty Ltd
Cnr Pyrmont Bridge Road
  and Bank Street
Pyrmont NSW 2009
Tel: (02) 9660 1611

Harris Farm Markets
Sydney Markets
Flemongton NSW 2140
Tel: (02) 9746 2055

Burlington Supermarkets
Chinatown Mall
Fortitude Valley QLD 4006
Tel: (07) 3216 1828

## UNITED KINGDOM

Good Harvest Fish Market
14 Newport Place
London WC2H 7PR
Tel: 020 7437 0712

Golden Gate Supermarket
16 Newport Place
London WC2H 7JS
Tel: 020 7437 6266

Hopewell Emporium
2f Dyne Road
London NW6 7XB
Tel: 020 7624 5473

Loon Fung Supermarket
42–44 Gerrard Street
London W1V 7LP
Tel: 020 7437 7332

Manila Supermarket
11–12 Hogarth Place
London SW5 0QT
Tel: 020 7373 8305

Miah, A. and Co
20 Magdalen Street
Norwich NR3 1HE
Tel: 01603 615395

New Peking Supermarket
59 Westbourne Grove
London W2 4UA
Tel: 020 7928 8770

Newport Supermarket
28–29 Newport Court
London WC2H 7PQ
Tel: 020 7437 2386

Rum Wong Supermarket
London Road
Guildford GU1 2AF
Tel: 01483 451568

S. W. Trading Ltd
Horn Lane
London SE10 0RT
Tel: 020 8293 9393

Sri Thai
56 Shepherd's Bush Road
London W6 7PH
Tel: 020 7602 0621

Talad Thai Ltd
320 Upper Richmond Road
London SW15 6TL
Tel: 020 8789 8084

Tawana
18–20 Chepstow Road
London W2 5BD
Tel: 020 7221 6316

Wang Thai Supermarket
101 Kew Road
Surrey TW9 2PN
Tel: 020 8332 2959

Wing Tai
11a Aylesham Centre
Rye Lane
London SE15 5EW
Tel: 020 7635 0714

Wing Yip
395 Edgware Road
London NW2 6LN
Tel: 020 7450 0422
*also at*
Oldham Road
Ancoats
Manchester M4 5HU
Tel: 0161 832 3215

*and*
375 Nechells Park Road
Nechells
Birmingham B7 5NT
Tel: 0121 327 3838

**Mail Order Companies**
Fiddes Payne Herbs
  and Spices Ltd
Unit 3B, Thorpe Way
Banbury
Oxfordshire OX16 8XL
Tel: 01295 253 888

Fox's Spices
Mason's Road
Stratford-upon-Avon
Warwickshire CV37 9XN
Tel: 01789 266 420

## UNITED STATES

Ai Hoa
860 North Hill Street
Los Angeles, CA 90026
Tel (213) 482-48

Asian Food Market
6450 Market Street
Upper Darby, PA 19082
Tel: (610) 352-4433

Asian Foods, Etc.
1375 Prince Avenue
Atlanta, GA 30341
Tel: (404) 543-8624

Asian Foods Ltd.
260-280 West Lehigh Avenue
Philadelphia, PA 19133
Tel: (215) 291-9500

Asian Market
2513 Stewart Avenue
Las Vegas, NV 89101
Tel: (702) 387-3373

Asian Market
18815 Eureka Road
South Gate, MI 48195
Fax: (734) 246-4795
www.asianmarket.qpg.com

Augusta Market Oriental Foods
2117 Martin Luther King Jr.
    Boulevard
Altanta, GA 30901
Tel: (706) 722-4988

Bachri's Chili & Spice Gourmet
5617 Villa Haven
Pittsburgh, PA 15236
Tel: (412) 831-1131
Fax: (412) 831-2542

Bangkok Market
4757 Melrose Avenue
Los Angeles, CA 90029
Tel: (203) 662-7990

Bharati Food & Spice Center
6163 Reynolds Road Suite G
Morrow, GA 30340
Tel: (770) 961-9007

First Asian Food Center
3420 East Ponce De Leon
    Avenue
Scottsdale, GA 30079
Tel: (404) 292-6508

The House of Rice Store
3221 North Hayden Road
Scottsdale, AZ 85251
Tel: (480) 947-6698

Han Me Oriental Food & Gifts
2 E. Derenne Avenue
Savannah, GA 31405
Tel: (912) 355-6411

Hong Tan Oriental Food
2802 Capitol Street
Savannah, GA 31404
Tel: (404) 233-9184

Huy Fong Foods Inc.
5001 Earle Avenue
Rosemead, CA 91770
Tel: (626) 286-8328
Fax: (626) 286-8522

Khanh Tam Oriental Market
4051 Buford Highway NE
Atlanta, GA 30345
Tel: (404) 728-0393

May's American Oriental Market
422 West University Avenue
Saint Paul, MN 55103
Tel: (651) 293-1118

Modern Thai Incorporated
135 Yacht Club Way #210
Hypuluxo, FL 33462
Tel: (888) THAI-8888

Norcross Oriental Market
6062 Norcross-Tucker Road
Chamblee, GA 30341
Tel: (770) 496-1656

Oriental Grocery
11827 Del Amo Boulevard
Cerritos, CA 90701
Tel: (310) 924-1029

Oriental Market
670 Central Park Avenue
Yonkers, NY 10013
(212) 349-1979

The Oriental Pantry
423 Great Road
Acton, MA 01720
Tel: (978) 264-4576

Saigon Asian Market
10090 Central Avenue
Biloxi, MS 39532
Tel: (228) 392-8044
Fax: (228) 392-8039
www.saigonor.qpg.com

Siam Market
27266 East Baseline Street
Highland, CA 92346
Tel: (909) 862-8060

Thai Market
3297 Las Vegas Boulevard
Las Vegas, NV 89030
Tel: (702) 643-8080

Thai Market
916 Harrelson Street
Fort Walton Beach, FL 32547
Tel: (904) 863-2013

Thai Number One Market
5927 Cherry Avenue
Long Beach, CA 90805
Tel: (310) 422-6915

Thai-Lao Market
1721 West La Palma Avenue
Anaheim, CA 92801
Tel: (714) 535-2656

Unimart American
    and Asian Groceries
1201 Howard Street
San Francisco, CA 94103
Tel: (415) 431-0362

**Publisher's Acknowledgements**
We would like to thank the following people and organizations for their invaluable help in the creation of this book: Charles Bradley, Pat Checkley (Tourist Authority of Thailand), Jonathan Hart, Chris Lee, Alissra Sinclair-Knopp (Language and Culture Consultant, The Thai Consulting Group), The Tourist Authority of Thailand, The Thai Embassy and a special thank you to Prisana Smith of the Tam Nak Thai Restaurant, 50–54 Westow Hill, London, SE19 1RX.
    We would like to thank Magimix UK and New Classic Limited for the generous loan of equipment used in the photographs in this book.

# INDEX